Pure Gold
Rock & Roll
Trivia Questions

Published by
Historical Publications, Inc.
15705 Hilcroft
Austin, Texas 78717-5331
(512) 255-4786
Fax: 255-4789
E-Mail: histpub@ix.netcom.com

ISBN # 1-881825-04-3
Library of Congress Catalog Card # 94-78290

Where to find it . . .

Dedication v

Foreword vii

Credits ix

Mr. Tom Moffatt x

How to keep score xi

Trivia Questions 1

My Days at Superstation KILT-A.M. 50

Special Bonus Elvis Section .70

Behind The Scenes . . . Beatles 86

The Night I Met The Beach Boys 94

My Days as a Rock 'n' Roll "Superstar" 103

The Shirelles Owe Me One 130

Meet Mr. Johnny Mathis 142

Trivia Answers 161

Index 179

Page iii

PURE GOLD ROCK & ROLL TRIVIA

Contents

. . . to Pat Clarke

    This book is gratefully dedicated to my friend, Pat Clarke who maintains the most positive attitude toward life, love and rock and roll that I have ever witnessed. It is a true honor to work with him. Pat is a much needed inspiration . . . I think we ought to elect him President and I'm not kidding!

Dedication

. . . from the author.

This is trivia! It is fun stuff! Several answers will differ from those in reputable trivia books simply because I asked the artist him or herself and went by what they told me. In researching the book I found that you can look up four questions in four books and come up with at least three different answers. Thus, in putting this book together, I have relied whenever possible on first hand knowledge.

The interviews are paraphrased.

This book is great for parties, DJs, reunions, car trips, lonely nights by the lava lamp . . . etc. The idea really hit me when I was in a car with a 23 year old girl, her mother and a 19 year old young man. I would ask a question and EVERYBODY KNEW THEY KNEW THE ANSWER! I thought: "Hold it here. How come a 19 year old guy is interested in Elvis trivia? And what am I doing in the car with a 23 year old girl?" Oh yeah . . . my wife of 25 years was there too. Whew! Then it dawned on me. Because the music of the '50's, '60's, and '70's is innocent and fun, a whole new generation is listening.

I thought this would be a simple task. Wrong. Making it interesting yet not too difficult was work. I just hope you have as much fun with it as I have. Most importantly I

hope you will never forget . . . this is trivia! If we begin to take it too seriously we miss the point. However the answers in this book have been checked and double checked and when there was a discrepancy, the question was omitted. Each question is rated according to its difficulty. Keep score, see who wins, and no cheating allowed. Yo.

Have fun. God bless you and goodnight.

Ron Foster–Captain Trivia

Foreword

Thanks to . . .

ABC Radio for their support in many ways.

Cash Case–Cover Design

David Nielsen–Book Design, Layout and Typesetting

The Beatles, Elvis Presley . . . and all others who made rock and roll history.

Terrie Johnson for the use of her Beatle photographs.

And thanks to:

Jon & June Wright	*Claire Bond*
Karen Ditto	*Beth Strange*

Thanks to the following for the use of their annuals for photographs:

Stephen F. Austin State University
Hillsborough High School
Brevardier High School
Texas City High School
University of Houston
University of Tampa

MR. TOM MOFFATT

A very special "thank you" to our good friend, Tom Moffatt for allowing us to publish exclusive pictures of Tom with some of rock's biggest superstars including Elvis. Debbie and I first met Tom on our second trip to the Hawaiian Islands. He always saw to it that we got to see the shows he was bringing to the islands and they were all fantastic.

Tom has had more influence on the music in Hawaii than probably any other individual not only through his Production Company, but in his many years behind the microphone as Hawaii's favorite DJ. When I mentioned this book to him he simply offered the pictures for us to use. A few days later I got them in the mail. His address is included. Whenever you are in Hawaii, check out any show "presented by" Tom Moffatt. If it's a Tom Moffatt production, it's got to be good! He is a first class guy all the way and so are the acts he represents. The following pages attest to his popularity in the '50's and the fact that he let us use them shows just what kind of guy he remains in the 1990's. Thanks Tom!

Tom Moffatt Productions, Inc.
The Penthouse
1232 Waimanu Street
Honolulu, Hawaii 96814

. . . can be fun

We've found the most fun way to keep track of your score is to simply mark down the number of each question with your answer next to it. When the party is over – whether or not you've completed the book in whole or part – check your answers contained in the back of the book. You will need to establish a prize for the winner, I have some really good ideas, but I'll leave that for your imagination.

Handicapps

Age: **1-20** 100 Points
    20-30 50 Points
    31-40 25 Points
    40+ 0 points

This way, you automatically win if you are under 20 and only play a few pages at a time. Anyone receiving a perfect score (without cheating) receives a night on the town paid for by his or her spouse or designated other. Fair enough? Have fun!!

Scoring

Score Card for:_____

Question/Answer	Question/Answer	Question/Answer
/	/	/
/	/	/
/	/	/
/	/	/
/	/	/
/	/	/
/	/	/
/	/	/
/	/	/
/	/	/
/	/	/
/	/	/
/	/	/
/	/	/
/	/	/
/	/	/
/	/	/
/	/	/

PURE GOLD ROCK & ROLL TRIVIA

Scoring

This page may be photocopied and used again and again and . . .

Score Card for:_____

Question/Answer	Question/Answer	Question/Answer
/	/	/
/	/	/
/	/	/
/	/	/
/	/	/
/	/	/
/	/	/
/	/	/
/	/	/
/	/	/
/	/	/
/	/	/
/	/	/
/	/	/
/	/	/
/	/	/
/	/	/
/	/	/
/	/	/

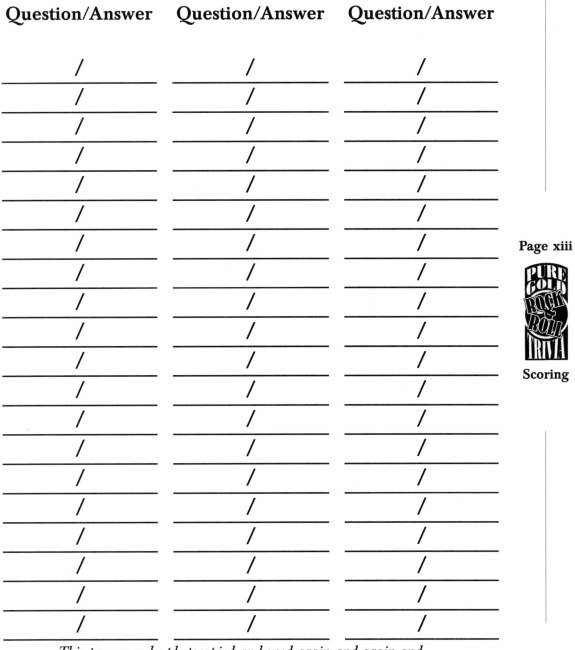

Page xiii

Scoring

This page may be photocopied and used again and again and . . .

(1)   Q: Is there really a Dead
       Man's Curve and if so, where
       is it located?

       A. *Dead Man's Curve was discovered by*
          Brian Wilson while at the beach at
          Santa Monica.
       B. *Dead Man's Curve is pure fiction.*
       C. *Dead Man's Curve is near U.C.L.A.*
       D. *Dead Man's Curve is a line from a*
          Clark Gable movie.
       Score: 7 points

(2)   Q: Who was the most famous
       graduate of Humes High
       School in Memphis?

       A. *Elvis Presley*
       B. *Jerry Lee Lewis*
       C. *Carl Perkins*
       D. *Dorsey Burnette*
       Score: 6 points

World's 1st and largest whoopie cushion
discovered by accident in 1954.

Questions

(3)   Q: Who wrote and originally
       recorded "Louie, Louie"?

       A. *Richard Berry wrote it, and the Raiders were the first to record it.*
       B. *Richard Berry wrote it, and the Kingsmen were the first to record it.*
       C. *Paul Revere wrote it, and the Raiders were the first to record it.*
       D. *Richard Berry wrote it, and was the first to record it.*
       Score: 8 points

(4)   Q: True or False? Glen Campbell played guitar on "Mr.
       Tambourine Man."
       Score: 4 points

(5)   Q: What is that audible "clink" near the
       end of Elvis's "Are You Lonesome
       Tonight"?

       A. *A cymbal was dropped in the men's room.*
       B. *A small bird landed in a window.*
       C. *Jerry Lee Lewis put a coin in a soda machine.*
       D. *Colonel Parker was counting his change and dropped a*
          penny. While bending down to retrieve it, he slipped.
       Score: 7 points

(6) **Q: What Beatle song is sung in the highest octave and who sings lead on it?**
A. *"You Can't Do That"-George*
B. *"I'm Down"-Paul*
C. *"Rock and Roll Music"-John*
D. *"Twist and Shout"-John*
Score: 4 points

(7) **Q: According to a 1989 interview with Ron Foster, where does Question Mark of ? and The Mysterians say he is from?**
A. *Mexico City*
B. *New Orleans*
C. *Los Angeles*
D. *The Planet Mars*
Score: 7 points

(8) **Q: Who played kettle drums on the Shirelles' classic hit "Will You Still Love Me Tomorrow"?**
A. *Glen Campbell*
B. *Little Eva*
C. *Carole King*
D. *Hal Blaine*
Score: 5 points

(9) **Q: What is considered to be the Beatles' first country sounding song?**
A. *"I Don't Want to Spoil the Party"*
B. *"Honey Don't"*
C. *"I'll Cry Instead"*
D. *"Act Naturally"*
Score: 7 points

Gee! That must hurt.

(10) **Q: Dion was first influenced by what famous singer?**
A. *Chuck Berry*
B. *Little Richard*
C. *Hank Williams, Sr.*
D. *George Jones*
Score: 8 points

Ron Foster backstage with Rudy Martinez, ? of "? and the Mysterians" of "96 Tears" fame. Maybe he is serious about the Mars thing.

Questions

(11)　Q: On which song does George Harrison seem to portray all world religions as one?

A. *"Imagine"*
B. *"My Sweet Lord"*
C. *"She's Leaving Home"*
D. *"Give Me Peace"*
Score: 5 points

(12)　Q: Mike Love and Brian Wilson wrote it, the Beach Boys recorded it, but someone else had the hit on it. Name that song.

A. *"Drag City"*
B. *"Surf City"*
C. *"Celebrate"*
D. *"Little Honda"*
Score: 7 points

(13) **Q: What famous sixties singer wrote the classic hit "He's A Rebel"?**
A. *Gene Pitney*
B. *Leon Russell*
C. *Marvin Gaye*
D. *Neil Sedaka*
Score: 8 points

(14) **Q: What group sang "He's A Rebel?"**
A. *The Supremes*
B. *The Chiffons*
C. *The Crystals*
D. *The Blossoms*
Score: 10 points

5 bonus points if you can name this person in 5 seconds.
Ready! Go. Answer Backwards: Noxin Drahcir

(15) **Q: Lulu's only big hit came from what motion picture?**
A. *"Camelot"*
B. *"To Sir With Love"*
C. *"Help!"*
D. *"Mr. Georgie"*
Score: 3 points

(16) **Q: What was Marvin Gaye's first #1 single?**
A. *"I Heard It Through the Grapevine"*
B. *"Shop Around"*
C. *"Doggin' Around"*
D. *"Let's Get It On"*
Score: 7 points

(17) **Q: Name Motown's first big hit.**
A. *"Shop Around"*
B. *"Little Darlin'"*
C. *"I Heard It Through the Grapevine"*
D. *"My Guy"*
Score: 6 points

Huge Profits! More Money!

(18) **Q: Dion was a heroin addict and alcoholic. How did he manage to turn his life around?**
A. *He quit cold turkey.*
B. *He became a Christian.*
C. *Pat Boone talked him "down".*
D. *He became a Muslim.*
Score: 7 points

(19) Q: **Which Beatle song starts out with the National Anthem of France?**
A. *"All You Need Is Love"*
B. *"Yellow Submarine"*
C. *"The Long and Winding Road"*
D. *"Hey Jude"*
Score: 3 points

(20) Q: **Who sang lead on the Beach Boys' "Barbara Ann"?**
A. *Carl Wilson*
B. *Brian Wilson*
C. *Dean Torrence*
D. *Jan Dean*
Score: 6 points

(21) Q: **Who was the subject of Stevie Wonder's "You Haven't Done Nothin' Yet"?**
A. *His ex-girlfriend, Mary Wilson*
B. *His father*
C. *Richard Nixon*
D. *Fidel Castro*
Score: 7 points

"So doctor, tell me about your tests with tobacco?"

Light my Fire!

(22) Q: Who wrote Rare Earth's "Get Ready (For Love)"?
A. *The song was a Bo Diddley standard.*
B. *Twenty-two year old, Marvin Gaye*
C. *Twenty-six year old, Smokey Robinson*
D. *Brian Wilson*
Score: 4 points

(23) Q: Before Ruby Nash joined the Romantics as their lead singer, the four men who made up the group were known as what?
A. *The Four Tops (litigation brought the name change)*
B. *The Four Jesters*
C. *The Temptations*
D. *The Supremes*
Score: 8 points

Questions

(24) Q: What song from 1961 was already being played on the radio as the "Pick of the Week" before the singer even got home from the studio after recording it?
A. *"Tossin' and Turnin'"-Bobby Lewis*
B. *"Moody River"-Pat Boone*
C. *"Let's Twist Again"-Chubby Checker*
D. *"The Twist"-Chubby Checker*
Score: 9 points

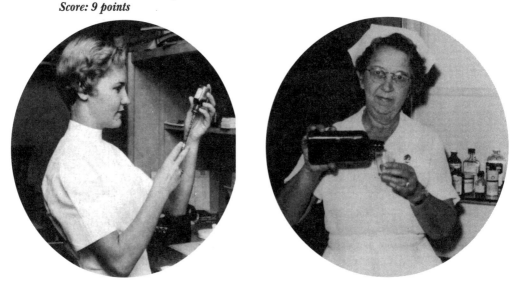

This explains why most of us never got sick at school!

(25) **Q: What was Elvis's first number one single . . . in Britain?**
A. "Hound Dog"
B. "Don't Be Cruel"
C. "All Shook Up"
D. "Love Me Tender"
Score: 9 points

(26) **Q: Which song's lyrics make it the oldest #1 song of the rock era?**
A. "Mr. Tambourine Man"
B. "It's All In The Game"
C. "Blue Moon"
D. "Turn, Turn, Turn"
Score: 8 points

(27) **Q: Which #1 single of 1961 is one of the most successful by a solo male vocalist of the entire rock era. It was #1 for an incredible 7 weeks!**
A. "Moody River"
B. "Tossin' and Turnin'"
C. "The Twist"
D. "Mother-in-Law"
Score: 10 points

Questions

(28) **Q: Which #1 song of 1968 expressed the emotional loss the writer felt after the tragic losses of Reverend Martin Luther King, Jr. and Senator Bobby Kennedy?**
A. "People Got to Be Free"
B. "Colour My World"
C. "Abraham, Martin, and John"
D. "War"
Score: 8 points

(29) **Q: According to chart action, what was the most successful Beatle's single?**
A. "Hey Jude"
B. "I Wanna Hold Your Hand"
C. "She Loves You"
D. "Twist and Shout"
Score: 6 points

(30) Q: **What song did the Supremes introduce on the Ed Sullivan Show and by discarding their glamorous outfits, make-up and wigs, and instead opt for sweat shirts, cut-offs and bare feet?**
A. *"The Happening"*
B. *"Love Child"*
C. *"Baby Love"*
D. *"Where Did Our Love Go"*
Score: 6 points

(31) Q: **What song did Tommy James say gave the Shondells their "own sound"?**
A. *"Sweet Cherry Wine"*
B. *"Crystal Blue Persuasion"*
C. *"Hanky Panky"*
D. *"Crimson and Clover"*
Score: 8 points

(32) Q: **What famous country singer joined Elvis for back up vocals on "Suspicious Minds"?**
A. *George Strait*
B. *Tammy Wynette*
C. *Ronnie Milsap*
D. *Conway Twitty*
Score: 7 points

Questions

(33) Q: **What was the first white girl group to have a #1 song on the charts?**
A. *The Angels*
B. *The Dixie Cups*
C. *The Sweet Inspirations*
D. *Kathy Young and the Innocents*
Score: 9 points

(34) Q: **Who did they call "The Genius" when he was only 12 years old.**
A. *Ray Charles*
B. *Ron Foster*
C. *Stevie Wonder*
D. *Smokey Robinson*
Score: 3 points

"Hello. Have a seat. The doctor will have your new glasses ready in a jiff. Ha ha ha."

(35) **Q: What was the Fleetwood's second #1 single?**
A. *"Come Softly to Me"*
B. *"Twilight Time"*
C. *"Hamburger"*
D. *"Mr. Blue"*
Score: 5 points

Helmets in 1954 gave as much protection as lip gloss.

(36) **Q: What was the only #1 song of the rock era to be written by a vice president of the United States?**
A. *"It's All In The Game"*
B. *"I'll Be Missing You"*
C. *"(We Did It) My Way"*
D. *"The Name Game"*
Score: 8 points

(37) **Q: Name the Vice President who wrote "It's All In The Game."**
A. *Garney "Snuff" Wilcox*
B. *Gerald Ford*
C. *Charles Gates Dowes*
D. *Edward E. Brennah*
Score: 10 points

(38) **Q: What was the first group of the rock era to become a "One Hit Wonder"?**
A. *The Elegants*
B. *The Hollywood Argyles*
C. *The Trashmen*
D. *The Rays*
Score: 8 points

(39) **Q: Which male vocalist of the rock era was named after silent screen actor Harold Lloyd?**
A. *Conway Twitty*
B. *Brian Wilson*
C. *Sonny Bono*
D. *Lloyd Price*
Score: 7 points

(40) Q: What do Frankie Avalon, Bobby Rydell, James Darren, Chubby Checker, Fabian and Dick Clark's "American Bandstand" all have in common?
A. *They were all born in Philadelphia.*
B. *They all came from the streets of the Bronx.*
C. *They were all born on the same day.*
D. *They were all on the cover of "Sgt. Pepper".*
Score: 7 points

(41) Q: Which Elvis song spent more consecutive weeks on the pop charts than any other Presley song?
A. *"Suspicious Minds"*
B. *"Jailhouse Rock"*
C. *"In the Ghetto"*
D. *"All Shook Up"*
Score: 8 points

(42) Q: Who was the most successful male hit maker of 1957?
A. *Elvis Presley*
B. *Jerry Lee Lewis*
C. *Pat Boone*
D. *Little Richard*
Score: 8 points

(43) Q: How long did Johnny Mathis's "Johnny's Greatest Hits" LP stay on the charts?
A. *Almost 11 months*
B. *One year*
C. *Ten years*
D. *15 years*
Score: 9 points

Mr. Tom Moffatt and Frankie Avalon

(44) Q: About whom was it written: "Those harmonic hicks are like all other Rock 'N' Roll stars . . . a flash or two and then they'll crawl back to the farms where they belong"?
A. *The Everly Brothers*
B. *Tom and Jerry (who later became Simon and Garfunkle)*
C. *Sam and Dave*
D. *Dale and Grace*
Score: 9 points

(45) Q: 1959 was the biggest year ever for instrumentals with 28 entering the national top 40. Which of the following was the most popular of those 28?
A. *"Sleepwalk"-Santo and Johnny*
B. *"The Happy Organ"-Dave "Baby" Cortez*
C. *"Red River Rock"-Johnny and the Hurricanes*
D. *"Quiet Village"-Martin Denny*
Score: 9 points

(46) Q: Who played piano on Bobby Darin's smash hit "Dream Lover"?
A. *Elton John*
B. *Liberace*
C. *Neil Sedaka*
D. *Leon Russell*
Score: 5 points

(47) Q: What was the first act to appear on television's "American Bandstand"?
A. *Danny and the Juniors*
B. *Frankie Avalon*
C. *The Chordettes*
D. *The Diamonds*
Score: 10 points

Questions

(48) Q: Which number one hit in America was completely banned in England the year it was released?
A. *"Louie, Louie"*
B. *"Rhapsody in the Rain"*
C. *"Teen Angel"*
D. *"Jailhouse Rock"*
Score: 8 points

(49) Q: What male singer had the most songs in the pop Top 10 between 1964 and 1974 in America?
A. *Elvis Presley*
B. *Fats Domino*
C. *Marvin Gaye*
D. *Paul McCartney*
Score: 7 points

(50) Q: What is Ringo Starr's real name?
A. Richard Star
B. Richard Starkley
C. Richard Starr
D. Richard Starkey
Score: 4 points

(51) Q: After their smash hit "At The Hop" what were Danny and the Juniors told to "Never Do Again?!!"
A. Chew gum on stage
B. Make another rock 'n' roll record
C. Appear on "American Bandstand" without written permission from their manager Ed Drusky
D. Appear on stage chewing tobacco
Score: 6 points

Questions

(52) Q: Name the first #1 Beatle song in the U.S. and their last as a group here.
A. "She Loves You" and "Let It Be"
B. "All My Love" and "Long and Winding Road"
C. "I Wanna Hold Your Hand" and "Long and Winding Road"
D. "I Saw Her Standing There" and "Hey Jude"
Score: 6 points

A little '60's fashion for ya!

(53) Q: Who wrote "Pretty Little Angel Eyes" for Curtis Lee, "Come A Little Bit Closer" for Jay and the Americans and the theme for the TV show "Where The Action Is"?
A. *Paul Anka*
B. *Tommy Boyce and Bobby Hart*
C. *Neil Sedaka*
D. *Curtis Lee*
Score: 5 points

(54) Q: What do Donna Summer, Dion, Roger McGuinn, Bob Dylan, Glen Campbell, Barry McGuire, Sam The Sham, Noel Paul Stookey, Van Morrison and Little Richard all have in common?
A. *They were all on the cover of "Sgt. Pepper".*
B. *They were all "All School Favorites".*
C. *They are all born again Christians.*
D. *They have all been elected to public office.*
Score: 6 points

(55) Q: Who was the writer and producer of the Murmaids' "Popsicles, Icicles"?
A. *Gene Pitney*
B. *David Gates*
C. *Neil Sedaka*
D. *Phil Spector*
Score: 7 points

(56) Q: What was the first group to play electronically amplified folk music and were known as the creators of Folk Rock?
A. *Peter, Paul and Mary*
B. *The Highwaymen*
C. *The Kingston Trio*
D. *The Byrds*
Score: 9 points

Questions

(57) **Q: What is considered to be John Lennon's first ballad?**
A. *"Michelle"*
B. *"If I Fell"*
C. *"Girl"*
D. *"Yesterday"*
Score: 9 points

(58) **Q: Who is Michael Leibowitz**
A. *Tiny Tim*
B. *Manfred Mann*
C. *Jim Morrison*
D. *Davy Jones*
Score: 7 points

(59) **Q: Who had the nickname "Motormouth"?**
A. *Little Richard*
B. *Billy Stewart*
C. *Billy Bland*
D. *Bobby Bland*
Score: 8 points

Questions

A Dipstick

(60) **Q: What do Steven Stills, Danny Hinton and John Sebastion all have in common?**
A. *They all auditioned to be Monkeys.*
B. *They were all on the cover of "Sgt. Pepper".*
C. *They are all exactly 5' 8" and were born on the same day.*
D. *They all graduated from Washington High School in Philadelphia.*
Score: 7 points

(61) **Q: Who sang lead vocals for the group Them on their hit version of "Gloria"?**
A. *Van Morrison*
B. *Sam the Sham*
C. *Billy Stewart*
D. *Buddy Balox*
Score: 4 points

"Let's see. 'Bates Motel' next exit. At last!"

Questions

(62) **Q: Who are Ray Dorset, Colin Earl, Michael Cale, Paul King, John Cook, Robert Daisley and David Bidwell?**
A. *The other members of the group Them.*
B. *The group Mungo Jerry.*
C. *The group Norman Greenbaum.*
D. *The group Shadows of Knight.*
Score: 8 points

(63) **Q: What does Olivia Newton John's first hit have in common with the Byrd's first hit?**
A. *They were both written by Bob Dylan.*
B. *They were both recorded the same day in the same studio.*
C. *They were both exactly 2:27 long.*
D. *They were both #1 on the same day one week apart.*
Score: 5 points

(64) **Q: How did the O'Jays get their name?**
A. *While thinking of a name for the group they noticed a bluejay which had landed in a nearby tree.*
B. *In honor of Eddie O'Jay, a Cleveland DJ who helped them get started.*
C. *In honor of the Big Bopper, J.P. Richardson.*
D. *In honor of the group's founder, Edmund O'Jay.*
Score: 8 points

(65) Q: What is significant about January 8, 1935 in rock history?

A. *The bass guitar was invented on that date by Edward F. Bass, the F. standing for Fender.*

B. *Elvis was born on that date.*

C. *Jerry Lee Lewis was born on that date.*

D. *It is the date of the first "official" blues recording.*

Score: 3 points

(66) Q: What do The Rascals and Joey Dee and the Starliners have in common?

A. *For several years they toured together in an oldies show.*

B. *The Rascals were a spin off from Joey Dee's band.*

C. *They both had hit versions of "The Peppermint Twist".*

D. *Joey Dee was the lead singer at one time of both groups.*

Score: 6 points

(67) Q: He guarded the gate at Graceland, emptied the ashtrays at the Columbia Records studio in Nashville and he had a #1 worldwide hit. Who is he?

A. *Van Morrison*

B. *Billy Swan*

C. *Ray Stephens*

D. *Conway Twitty*

Score: 6 points

(68) Q: Approximately how much did it cost to record the #1 hit "96 Tears"?

A. *$5,000*

B. *$500*

C. *$50*

D. *$5*

Score: 8 points

(69) Q: What do the B. and the J. stand for in B.J. Thomas?

A. *Bobby John*

B. *Billy John*

C. *Billy Joe*

D. *Bobby Joe*

Score: 2 points

"Do NOT put finger in big machine!"

(70) **Q: Who is Herbert Khaury?**
A. *Tom Jones*
B. *Tiny Tim*
C. *Van Morison*
D. *Sam the Sham*
Score: 6 points

(71) **Q: What were the Monkeys' first and last hit singles?**
A. *"Last Train to Clarksville" and "Valerie"*
B. *"Daydream Believer" and "Valerie"*
C. *"Last Train to Clarksville" and "Pleasant Valley Sunday"*
D. *"I'm a Believer" and "Pleasant Valley Sunday"*
Score: 8 points

(72) **Q: What was the "Answer" song to "Blueberry Hill"?**
A. *"Cherry Hill Park"*
B. *"Let's Go"*
C. *"Hills and Bells"*
D. *"The Three Bells"*
Score: 10 points

(73) **Q: What is Chubby Checker's real name?**
A. *Ernest Tubb*
B. *Ernest Evans*
C. *Bob Morley*
D. *Ed Clyde*
Score: 6 points

(74) **Q: On which Beatle song did Paul McCartney make a very obvious mistake which was left on the record?**
A. *"She Loves You"*
B. *"Ob La Di Ob La Da"*
C. *"Love Me Do"*
D. *"Hey Jude"*
Score: 9 points

"Wonder what happens if I put my finger in this big machine?"

Questions

(75) **Q: Before they were the Coasters they were the:**
A. *They were always the Coasters.*
B. *Coastliners*
C. *Robins*
D. *Miracles*
Score: 7 points

(76) **Q: Who is Reginald Kenneth Dwight?**
A. *Archie Bell of the Drells*
B. *Elton John*
C. *Sam the Sham*
D. *Bobby "Boris" Pickett*
Score: 6 points

(77) **Q: Who was Little Sunny Wilson?**
A. *Jackie Wilson*
B. *Wilson Pickett*
C. *Carl Wilson*
D. *Hank Ballard*
Score: 7 points

Questions

Our very own Pat Clarke with Hank Ballard–the man who wrote and originally recorded "The Twist".

(78) **Q: Who originally wrote and recorded "The Twist"?**
A. *Hank Ballard wrote it; Chubby Checker was the first to record it.*
B. *Hank Ballard wrote it; The Diamonds were the first to record it.*
C. *Hank Ballard was the first to record the song he wrote.*
D. *Chubby Checker wrote it and was the first to record it.*
Score: 9 points

(79) **Q: Name the first British group to have a #1 hit in America**
A. *The Beatles*
B. *The Stones*
C. *The Tornadoes*
D. *Jerry and the Pacemakers*
Score: 9 points

(80) **Q: Who played piano on the hit "Monster Mash"?**
A. *Leon Russell*
B. *Neil Sedaka*
C. *Bobby "Boris" Pickett*
D. *Gene Pitney*
Score: 9 points

(81) Q: Who sings the "Oonka-Chunkas" in the background on Johnny Preston's "Running Bear"?
A. J.P. Richardson - the Big Bopper
B. George Jones
C. Aaron Neville
D. Ernie K. Doe
Score: 10 points

(82) Q: Why did Dick Clark suggest that someone else cut the Hank Ballard song, "The Twist"?
A. He managed Chubby Checker and wanted to get a piece of the action.
B. Hank Ballard was scheduled to appear on "Bandstand" but didn't show up for some reason.
C. Dick thought the song would be good for "Bandstand" but didn't like Hank Ballard's version.
D. Quite frankly, Dick Clark and Hank Ballard never got along. This was Dick's way of getting even. To this day he regrets it.
Score: 10 points

(83) Q: Who did Dick Clark first suggest should cut another version of "The Twist"?
A. Hank Ballard
B. Chubby Checker
C. Danny and The Juniors
D. The Diamonds
Score: 10 points

Never let someone take a picture of you dancing.

Questions

(84) Q: After three weeks of demonstrating "The Twist" on a promotional campaign, what did Chubby Checker accidentally drop?
A. While performing at a dance at a Philadelphia High School, Chubby dropped his wedding ring which has never been found.
B. Chubby dropped 20 pounds.
C. Chubby dropped 30 pounds.
D. Chubby dropped a watch that Dick Clark had given him. It shattered on the stage, however, Chubby just kept on twistin'!
Score: 7 points

(85) Q: During a 1961 audition for Decca records in London, George Harrison sang "The Shiek of Araby" as Brian Epstein predicted to the label executives that someday the group would be bigger than Elvis. After hearing George sing, what was Decca's response to Brian?

A. *The Beatles were escorted out of the building-no deal.*
B. *They were invited back for a second audition, but by that time were stars on their own.*
C. *The Beatles were signed on the spot and placed on a smaller subsidiary, Vee Jay.*
D. *The boys sang several more songs before being turned down.*
Score: 9 points

Questions

(86) Q: What was the most important female pop group of the early sixties?

A. *The Marvelettes*
B. *The Supremes*
C. *The Shangrilas*
D. *The Shirelles*
Score: 9 points

(87) Q: True or False? "The Twist" provided a landfall for chiropractors?
Score: 3 points

7-UP "FLOAT

SEVEN-UP AND ICE CREAM

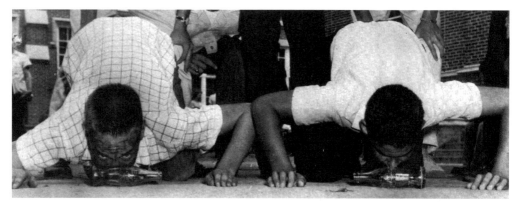

Losers of spin the bottle!

(88) **Q: What was "West Side Story" based on?**
   A. It was an updated version of "Virginia Wolfe".
   B. It was an updated version of Shakespeare's "Romeo and Juliet".
   C. It was based on Johnny Mathis's first girlfriend Maria-his years in the gangs.
   D. It was based on "Camelot".
   Score: 8 points

(89) **Q: What were two things that Dee Dee Sharp did not like about her hit "Mashed Potato Time"?**
   A. She thought the song was too short and did not like the beat.
   B. She wanted her name to be listed as Dee Sharp and she did not like the take.
   C. She did not like her hairdo on the album and hated her dress.
   D. She did not like mashed potatoes or dancing to the song.
   Score: 8 points

(90) **Q: What was the original working title of the Tymes "So Much in Love"?**
   A. "Walking in the Sand"
   B. "Kissing in the Picture Booth"
   C. "So Much in Love with You, Sandy"
   D. "The Stroll"
   Score: 9 points

The perfect answer.

(91) **Q: How much money did the Beach Boys' father, Murray, ask for their master recordings including their very first charted song "Surfin'"?**
   A. $10,000
   B. $1,000
   C. $100
   D. He gave it away.
   Score: 9 points

It's the real thing. Coke.

(92) **Q: What do "Walking in the Rain" by the Ronettes and "Rhythm of the Rain" by the Cascades have in common?**
   A. They are exactly the same length.
   B. The thunder and rain sound effects are identical.
   C. Each record contains exactly 776 grooves.
   D. Both records were originally released on blue vinyl.
   Score: 8 points

Page 22

PURE
GOLD
ROCK
&
ROLL
TRIVIA

Questions

(93) Q: **What was the Kinks most successful record?**
A. *"All Day and All of the Night"*
B. *"You Really Got Me"*
C. *"Tired of Waiting for You"*
D. *"Lola"*
Score: 9 points

(94) Q: **Carly Simon's "You're So Vain" was directed at several of the singer's old boyfriends, but mainly the song was intended for whom?**
A. *James Taylor*
B. *Julio Iglesias*
C. *Warren Beatty*
D. *Jack Nicholson*
Score: 5 points

(95) Q: **What was the estimated audience for Elvis Presley's "The Aloha Satellite Show" worldwide?**
A. *10 million*
B. *50 million*
C. *100 million*
D. *1 1/2 billion*
Score: 7 points

"Someday, that guy in the suit is gonna realize how silly he looks."

(96) Q: **She was one of six kids who slept in the same room, three to a bed, with a kerosene jar lighted to keep the insects away. She worked at Hudson's Department Store as a "Cafeteria Busy Girl." She walked to school with two neighborhood friends, Mary Wilson and Florence Ballard. Who is she?**
A. *Shirley Ellis*
B. *Dianna Ross*
C. *Barbara Streisand*
D. *Carly Simon*
Score: 6 points

(97) Q: Who is the guy in the picture to the right?
A. *George Bush*
B. *Ron Foster*
C. *Stevie Wonder*
D. *Smokey Robinson*
Score: 5 points

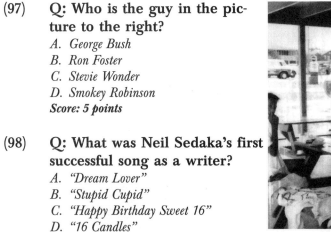

(98) Q: What was Neil Sedaka's first successful song as a writer?
A. *"Dream Lover"*
B. *"Stupid Cupid"*
C. *"Happy Birthday Sweet 16"*
D. *"16 Candles"*
Score: 9 points

(99) Q: How old was Franki Valli when "Sherry" went to #1?
A. *20*
B. *22*
C. *28*
D. *33*
Score: 9 points

Questions

George Bush on the campaign trail - University of Houston - 1968.

Astronaut Virgil I. Grissom

Astronaut Edward H. White

Astronaut Roger B. Chaffee

IN MEMORIAM

Died at Cape Kennedy on January 28, 1967

(100) Q: What was Johnny Mathis planning to do professionally if he had not become a successful singer?
A. *A hairdresser*
B. *A cook*
C. *An English or P.E. teacher*
D. *A truck driver*
Score: 6 points

(101) Q: What did the "New York Daily News" suggest be done with Rock and Roll dancing?
A. *". . . be banned"*
B. *". . . made illegal without parental consent"*
C. *". . . to be punishable by a fine of up to $100 . . ."*
D. *"destroyed . . . this is anarchy . . ."*
Score: 9 points

(102) Q: Which Beatle album is considered by most critics to be the "Best in terms of quality of most individual songs"?
A. *"Meet The Beatles"*
B. *"Revolver"*
C. *"Rubber Soul"*
D. *"Sgt. Pepper"*
Score: 10 points

(103) Q: John Lennon claimed that he wrote "about 70%" of the Lyrics on the song, however Paul said that John wrote about "half a line." Over which song did this unusual discrepancy occur?
A. *"Hey Jude"*
B. *"Yesterday"*
C. *"Eleanor Rigby"*
D. *"Yellow Submarine"*
Score: 10 points

In Memoriam

John Fitzgerald Kennedy
35th President of the United States
Born: May 29, 1917
Died: November 22, 1963

Questions

Ferris Beuller, Sr. is lying again . . .

"Honest, I'm sick. I can't come to school today."

Questions

(104) **Q: How many singles did the Four Seasons release in the 1950's?**
A. *0*
B. *1*
C. *5*
D. *This is a trick question.*
Score: 9 points

(105) **Q: What was Gerry of Gerry and the Pacemakers last name?**
A. *Tubb*
B. *Mercer*
C. *Marspen*
D. *Brithtenton*
Score: 6 points

(106) **Q: What was the name of Puff the Magic Dragon's little friend?**
A. *Jackie Paper*
B. *Jolley Paper*
C. *Johnny Paper*
D. *Joni Pepper*
Score: 4 points

He's not sick.

"Hello. Ferris please."

Questions

(107) **Q: What famous sixties group began in 1963 as an L.A. surf band called the "Nightriders"?**
A. *The Beach Boys*
B. *Jan and Dean*
C. *The Turtles*
D. *The Ventures*
Score: 8 points

(108) **Q: What was the first #1 single for producer Quincy Jones?**
A. *"To Know Him Is To Love Him"*
B. *"I Heard It Through the Grapevine" - Marvin Gaye*
C. *"I Heard It Through the Grapevine" - Gladys Knight*
D. *"It's My Party" - Leslie Gore*
Score: 7 points

"Just a moment."

"Ah oh. There's a foot on my plate."

Questions

(109)   Q: When a certain individual came on television, Elvis had a
         "bad" habit of pulling out the nearest gun and shooting out the
         screen. Of the choices below, who was this "talented" singer?
         A. Tiny Tim
         B. Bobby "Boris" Pickett
         C. Robert Goulet
         D. Pat Boone
         Score: 7 points

(110)   Q: About how much money does Ray Hilderbrand (Paul of Paul
         and Paula) receive yearly in royalties from "Hey Paula"?
         A. Ray does not receive further compensation.
         B. $10,000
         C. $21,900
         D. $100,000
         Score: 9 points

(111) **Q:** According to reliable sources, what famous half of what famous duo sang backup on the Ronettes' Hit "Be My Baby"?

A. *Cher*
B. *Paula (of Paul and Paula)*
C. *Paul Simon*
D. *Phil Evenly*
Score: 5 points

(112) **Q:** Johnny Maestro was the lead singer on "Sixteen Candles." On what other hit song did he sing lead with another group?

A. *"Young Girl"*
B. *"The Worst That Could Happen"*
C. *"Never My Love"*
D. *"Cherish"*
Score: 9 points

(113) **Q:** Name two male singers who were signed to recording contracts in 1958 more for their looks than their singing ability.

A. *Sonny Bono and Tiny Tim*
B. *Fabian and Frankie Avalon*
C. *Frankie Avalon and Pat Boone*
D. *Tab Hunter and James Dean*
Score: 8 points

This guy knows a Sadie Hawkins when he sees one!

Questions

(114) **Q:** Typically, what does Frankie Avalon ask the audience to do after a performance?

A. *He offers discounts on his beach movies with Annette which he offers to autograph for free.*
B. *To sing on the show while balancing a pitcher of soda on their head.*
C. *To come up to his room for a drink and conversation.*
D. *To buy a collection of his greatest hits which he will autograph.*
Score: 10 points

(115)   Q: What do Elvis, John Lennon, Farrah Fawcett, President Jimmy Carter and Senator Barry Goldwater all have in common?

A. They all officially reported UFO sightings.
B. They were all born on the same day of the week.
C. They were all on the cover of "Sgt. Pepper".
D. None of them were on the cover of "Sgt. Pepper".

Score: 9 points

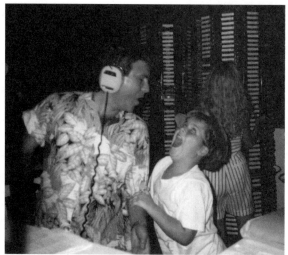

Ron, son Chance, back end of daughter Shawna. Is this fun or what?

Questions

Chance, Richard Byrd and Ron Foster. Richard knows more about rock 'n' roll trivia than all of us combined!

Actual radio broadcasting . . .

Questions

(116) Q: What famous group of the sixties had absolutely no success until they began to copy the style of Maurice Williams and the Zodiacs?
A. *Frankie Lymon and the Teenagers*
B. *The Rays*
C. *The Flamingos*
D. *The Four Seasons*
Score: 8 points

(117) Q: What famous rock star was a loyal supporter of Richard Nixon?
A. *Pat Boone*
B. *Wayne Newton*
C. *Elvis Presley*
D. *Bob Dylan*
Score: 5 points

(118) Q: How old was Freddie Cannon when "Tallahassee Lassie" hit the top 10?
A. *22*
B. *21*
C. *19*
D. *18*
Score: 8 points

(119) **Q: What did Colonel Parker reportedly insist country singer David Houston do prior to going on stage before Elvis in one of the King's Early concerts?**
   A. *Remain still and not mimic Elvis's body movements*
   B. *Shave his sideburns*
   C. *Remain on stage for a maximum of 15 minutes*
   D. *Make no reference to Elvis's upcoming induction*
   Score: 7 points

(120) **Q: Which fifties group is considered "the most original and inventive"?**
   A. *The Diamonds*
   B. *The Coasters*
   C. *Danny and The Juniors*
   D. *The Platters*
   Score: 8 points

Ron, Debbie and George Foreman. Heavy Weight Champion . . . Again . . . 1995 . . . WOW!

(121) **Q: True or false? Chuck Berry was almost 20 years old when he recorded "Roll Over Beethoven," "Sweet Little 16," and "Rock And Roll Music"?**
   Score: 6 points

"The Greatest" and Debbie

Questions

(122) Q: Who was a yodel-
ling hillbilly singer
with such groups as
"The Four Aces of
Western Swing" and
the "Saddlemen"
before going rock?
A. *Conway Twitty*
B. *Bill Haley*
C. *Buddy Holly*
D. *Jerry Lee Lewis*
Score: 9 points

Famed blues singer Lightnin' Hopkins in 1969

(123) Q: What was the
Beatles' best kept
secret?
A. *John Lennon was mar-*
ried when the group first
invaded the U.S.
B. *Paul McCartney had*
written articles in high
school against the "lazy
American youth".
C. *Pete Best was also on the*
plane, and the decision
between him and Ringo was still being contested.
D. *Ringo Starr was really from Australia.*
Score: 9 points

(124) Q: How many #1 songs has Little Richard charted?
A. *None*
B. *2*
C. *5*
D. *11*
Score: 3 points

(125) Q: Who were the backup singers on Little Eva's "Locomotion"?
A. *The Sweet Inspirations*
B. *The Chiffons*
C. *The Cookies*
D. *The Marvelettes*
Score: 9 points

The Lettermen sing for a packed crowd in 1969 (above) and 1968 (below).

(126)   Q: Who was the opening act for Bruce Channel when he toured Europe riding the success of "Hey Baby"?
A. Roy Orbison
B. Jerry Lee Lewis
C. The Rolling Stones
D. The Beatles
Score: 6 points

(127)   Q: To whom did Elvis say: "Look, if you are going to just sit there and stare at me all night, I'm going to bed"?
A. The first crowd for whom he performed in Las Vegas, 1969
B. The Beatles when they visited his California home
C. The audience at the Grand Ole Opry in 1955
D. Pricilla when they first dated
Score: 9 points

I . . . I . . .
Well . . . uh
Thank You
very much

(128)   Q: What group was put together to duplicate the tremendous success of the Kingston Trio?
A. The Kingsmen
B. Peter, Paul and Mary
C. The Smothers Brothers
D. The Mamas and Papas
Score: 8 points

(129)   Q: True or False? The Ronnettes made their professional debut with the Beatles in Candlestick Park in early 1964?
Score: 5 points

(130)   Q: Approximately how many records did "The Letter" by the Boxtops sell worldwide?
A. 25 million
B. 1 billion
C. 6 million
D. 4 million
Score: 10 points

(131) **Q: What is considered to be the flaw in the Beach Boys' classic hit "Good Vibrations"?**

A. *The song was considered much too long for its time and was slow in getting airplay.*

B. *Several of the harmonies are not on key.*

C. *Brian Wilson was never satisfied with the drum track which skips several beats.*

D. *The song was recorded in mono.*

Score: 9 points

(132) **Q: In what year did Rick Nelson drop the "y" from his name?**

A. *1959*

B. *1960*

C. *1961*

D. *1963 (though Rick had asked for the change in 1958)*

Score: 9 points

(133) **Q: What was the first record the Stones made?**

A. *"Satisfaction"*

B. *"Mother's Little Helper"*

C. *"Come On"*

D. *"My Helper"*

Score: 9 points

Ron Foster backstage with Carl Wilson of the Beach Boys. Carl sang the lead on many hits including "Good Vibrations." Yo Carl!

Questions

(134) **Q: What did Paula Anka, Brenda Lee and Chubby Checker all vow to do in 1963?**

A. *To spend more time at home with their families*

B. *To spend more time on the road*

C. *To slow down on the road—they were all issued speeding tickets that very year*

D. *They were all married that year*

Score: 9 points

(135) **Q: In what year did Sonny and Cher get married?**

A. *1964*

B. *1963*

C. *1962*

D. *1961*

Score: 9 points

(136) Q: Who played the bells on the Willows' fifties hit "Church Bells May Ring"?
A. Sonny Bono
B. Neil Sedaka
C. Pat Boone
D. 14 year old Dion
Score: 8 points

(137) Q: In what year did the FCC give its approval for FM stations to go stereo?
A. 1961
B. 1962
C. 1963
D. 1964
Score: 10 points

(138) Q: Which Rolling Stones' song utilizes full orchestration?
A. "As Tears Go By"
B. "Satisfaction"
C. "Mother's Little Helper"
D. This is a dumb trick question.
Score: 9 points

Debbie and Ron. That's Debbie with the sideburns.

(139) Q: What was the Supremes' first hit?
A. "Baby Love"
B. "Where Did Our Love Go"?
C. "The Happening"
D. "Someday We'll Be Together"
Score: 6 points

(140) Q: Who was the first musician to use strings on a rock 'n' roll record?
A. Tommy Roe
B. The Rolling Stones
C. Bill Haley
D. Buddy Holly
Score: 9 points

(141) Q: Who owns the rights to all Buddy Holly songs?
A. A trust fund set up in Holly's name
B. Paul McCartney
C. Bob Dylan
D. The rights were purchased in 1976 by the Grand Ole Opry.
Score: 7 points

(142) Q: How did Motown get its name?
A. From Smokey Robinson's name Smo-Mo
B. Marvin Gaye suggested the name.
C. It was taken from the word "more" referring to the beat.
D. From its home in Detroit which is called "motortown"
Score: 6 points

(143) Q: Who was the youngest female singer of the rock era to have a #1 single?
A. Brenda Lee
B. Little Peggy March
C. Connie Francis
D. Leslie Gore
Score: 9 points

(144) Q: Who played drums on the American version of "Love Me Do"?
A. Ringo Starr
B. Pete Best
C. Andy White
D. Hal Blaine
Score: 9 points

CONNIE FRANCIS M-G-M RECORDS STAR

An official Connie Francis Fan Club Card. Connie was the biggest female hit maker of the '50s.

Questions

I wish to be registered as an official member of the

CONNIE FRANCIS FAN CLUB

Name....................................

Address.................................

City........................State........

Note: In those days there was no zip code.

(145) **Q: Who wrote "My Guy" made famous by Mary Wells?**
A. *Mary Wells*
B. *Carole King*
C. *Smokey Robinson*
D. *Marvin Gaye*
Score: 9 points

(146) **Q: In a 68-week period that began on August 8, 1963, who was the only American artist or group to have a #1 single in Britain and what was the name of the song?**
A. *Elvis with "Crying in the Chapel"*
B. *Roy Orbison and his "Pretty Woman"*
C. *The Four Seasons with "Rag Doll"*
D. *Pat Boone bubbling with "Moody River"*
Score: 10 points

The original Mrs. Doubtfire

(147) **Q: Who was Mr. Nudy?**
A. *This is obviously a trick question–good grief!*
B. *This was Elvis's hairdresser.*
C. *Elvis's clothes designer.*
D. *He was a famous rock critic.*
Score: 5 points

(148) **Q: In 1957 The Everly Brothers had two million selling songs in a row with "Bye Bye Love" and "Wake Up Little Susie." Approximately how much money was each Everly getting paid for each performance after the songs made the charts?**
A. *$100*
B. *$250*
C. *$2,000*
D. *$3,000*
Score: 6 points

(149) Q: **What #1 song of the fifties was written in a men's room between Las Vegas performances?**
A. *"16 Candles"*
B. *"Little Darlin'"*
C. *"The Great Pretender"*
D. *"Hound Dog"*
Score: 10 points

(150) Q: **What was the first song of the rock era to utilize the "fuzz" or distorted guitar?**
A. *"Don't Worry"*
B. *"You Really Got Me"*
C. *"I Feel Fine"*
D. *"All Day and All of the Night"*
Score: 10 points

(151) Q: **What ever happened to the Alan Price Combo in 1962?**
A. *They changed their name to the Rolling Stones.*
B. *They changed their name to the Animals.*
C. *They changed their name to Joe Dee and the Starlighters.*
D. *They changed their name to the Turtles.*
Score: 9 points

Dancing with the invisible man.

(152) Q: **What was Pat Boone's last Top 10 hit?**
A. *"Speedy Gonzales"*
B. *"Moody River"*
C. *"Keep-a-Knockin'"*
D. *A remake of "Love Letters in the Sand"*
Score: 9 points

(153) Q: **Who played guitar on Dion's "The Wanderer"?**
A. *Mickey of Mickey and Sylvia ("Love is Strange")*
B. *Bo Diddley*
C. *Paul of Paul and Paula ("Hey Paula")*
D. *Dion*
Score: 10 points

(154) Q: **Which Beatles' song is Ringo most proud of when it comes to his drumming?**
A. *"She Loves You"*
B. *"Strawberry Fields"*
C. *"Rain"*
D. *"For the Benefit of Mr. Kite"*
Score: 9 points

Geared

(155) **Q: Who bought a Macon, Georgia radio station he had once shined shoes in front of?**
A. *Little Richard*
B. *Bobby Lewis*
C. *James Brown*
D. *Little Anthony*
Score: 9 points

(156) **Q: Elvis had a big hit with "Crying in the Chapel." Who had the original?**
A. *Darrell Glenn*
B. *June Valli*
C. *Rex Allen*
D. *Sonny Till and the Orioles*
Score: 10 points

"Don't look now, but we just skated into a trivia book."

(157) **Q: What happened to Garry Lewis in 1966, which to this day he will not discuss in interviews?**
A. *He had a falling out with Dean Martin.*
B. *He had a falling out with his dad, Jerry Lewis.*
C. *He was drafted and was not a happy camper.*
D. *He was arrested for possession of less than one ounce of marijuana.*
Score: 8 points

(158) **Q: What popular group of the late sixties was originally named the Hi Fi's?**
A. *Garry Lewis and the Playboys*
B. *The Foundations*
C. *The Fifth Dimension*
D. *The Archies*
Score: 10 points

(159) **Q: How many members originally made up Herb Alpert and the Tijuana Brass?**
A. *One*
B. *Two*
C. *Three*
D. *Four*
Score: 10 points

(160)   Q: What was the original title of "96 Tears"?

A. "Lookin' Down at your Love"
B. "77 Tears"
C. "69 Tears"
D. "I'm Lookin' Up at Your Love"

Score: 10 points

(161)   Q: What is significant about Johnny Rivers' hit "Seventh Son"?

A. Johnny Rivers was the seventh son of a seventh son.
B. Johnny recorded the song on the seventh day of the seventh month and got in on the seventh take.
C. When added together, the numbers 7 plus 7 plus 7 equaled Johnny's age at a time of the recording.
D. Johnny had been involved in a car accident in which he was declared legally dead. He "came back to life" thus the line "raised from the dead . . . drive the little girl's out of their head."

Score: 10 points

(162)   Q: In what year did Bob Dylan play Carnegie Hall?

A. 1977
B. 1967
C. 1961
D. Bob never played Carnegie Hall.

Score: 10 points

In the 60's, we ate sand. . .

. . . but back in the 50's we were more sophisticated.

(163) **Q: How many people attended Bob Dylan's 1961 Carnegie Hall appearance?**
A. 2,333
B. 10,333
C. 533
D. 53
Score: 10 points

(164) **Q: Who is Marie McDonald McLaughlyn?**
A. *Marie Osmond by her married name*
B. *Lulu*
C. *Diana Ross*
D. *Martha Reeves*
Score: 10 points

(165) **Q: What famous singer was fired from his job as a hospital orderly for singing in the hallways?**
A. *Otis Redding*
B. *Bobby "Boris" Pickett*
C. *Roy Orbison*
D. *Ernie K. Doe*
Score: 10 points

(166) **Q: What famous fifties singer inspired Tommy James?**
A. *Buddy Holly*
B. *Little Richard*
C. *Elvis Presley*
D. *Tommy Roe*
Score: 10 points

(167) **Q: What was Tommy Roe's biggest hit?**
A. *"Shiela"*
B. *"Sweet Pea"*
C. *"Dizzy"*
D. *"Everybody"*
Score: 8 points

"Sorry Jeanie, but I'm all booked!"

Burritos.

PURE GOLD ROCK & ROLL TRIVIA

Questions

(168) Q: What song was the inspiration for the Stones' "Honky Tonk Women"?

A. The Kleenex jingle
B. "Honky Tonkin'" by Hank Williams, Sr.
C. "I'm a Honky Tonk Man" by Johnny Horton
D. "Honky Tonk Part I and II" by Bill Doggett
Score: 8 points

(169) Q: According to Paul McCartney, what was the first song he ever wrote in which he had the words before the music?

A. "She Loves You"
B. "Yesterday"
C. "All My Lovin'"
D. "Michelle"
Score: 10 points

(170) Q: Which Elvis hit did he, at first, refuse to sing because he thought the words were dumb?

A. "Hard Headed Woman"
B. "Hound Dog"
C. "(I Want to Be Your) Teddybear"
D. "Stuck on You"
Score: 6 points

(171) Q: What was Petula Clark's first British release?

A. "A Little Sand Between My Toes"
B. "Putting on My Silver Slippers"
C. "My Ballerina Shoes"
D. "Putting Shoes on Lucy"
Score: 10 points

(172) Q: Name Motown's first male group to achieve a #1 single.

A. Smokey Robinson with "Shop Around"
B. Mary Wells with "My Guy"
C. The Temptations with "My Girl"
D. "I Can't Help Myself" by the Four Tops
Score: 10 points

Pat Clarke alongside the man they call "the Duke", an original member of the "Four Tops."

Questions

(173) Q: In 1964 who was playing backup guitar for the Isley Brothers at $30.00 a night?
A. *Jimi Hendrix*
B. *Glenn Campbell*
C. *Eric Clapton*
D. *Bo Diddley*
Score: 8 points

(174) Q: What song bumped "Hound Dog" and "Don't Be Cruel" out of its #1 position?
A. *"Love Me Tender"*
B. *"Whole Lotta Shakin'"*
C. *"Blue Suede Shoes"*
D. *"Great Balls of Fire"*
Score: 7 points

Anthony Perkins and Debbie look a little like brother and sister. Hmmm. Now I'll be afraid to shower.

(175) Q: Which of these singles was on the charts the longest?
A. *"Hey Jude"*
B. *"Don't Be Cruel"*
C. *"Rock Around the Clock"*
D. *"Love Letters in the Sand"*
Score: 8 points

(176) Q: Who did the whistling on song choice "D" from above?
A. *Pat Boone*
B. *Clyde McPhatter*
C. *Jimi Hendrix*
D. *Neil Sedaka*
Score: 10 points

Questions

(177) Q: What was Larry Williams doing professionally before becoming a singing star with "Bony Moronie"?
A. *He was a chicken plucker.*
B. *He was the valet for Lloyd Price.*
C. *He was Fats Domino's bass guitarist.*
D. *He was a hairdresser in Los Angeles.*
Score: 9 points

(178) Q: What was the first #1 record to use an electronic organ?
A. *"Runaway"*
B. *"96 Tears"*
C. *"The Happy Organ"*
D. *"Time Won't Let Me"*
Score: 9 points

(179) Q: In 1960, which way was Johnny Horton going to Alaska?
A. *North*
B. *South*
C. *East*
D. *West*
Score: 3 points

(180) Q: The group had about five minutes of expensive studio time left. So, rather than waste it, a song was written on the spot and recorded on the first take. Amazingly this became one of the biggest hits of one of the most popular groups of the sixties! Name that song and group!

A. "Sherry" by the Four Seasons
B. "Game of Love" by Wayne Fontanna and the Mindbenders
C. "Don't Say Nothin' Bad About My Baby" by the Cookies
D. "Soldier Boy" by the Shirelles
Score: 10 points

(181) Q: With the British invasion in full force by 1965, who was called by critics a "relic(s) of an earlier era"?

A. Elvis
B. The Beach Boys
C. The Four Seasons
D. All American groups and individual rock singers
Score: 9 points

(182) Q: What was the first #1 song of the rock era on the Epic label?

A. "Twist and Shout" by the Isley Brothers
B. "Shout" by the Isley Brothers
C. "Roses Are Red" by Bobby Vinton
D. "Walking in the Sand" by the Shangrilas
Score: 10 points

Questions

My Days As A
GoodTime 610 Man at
Superstation-KILT-AM

I considered my job at KILT-AM in Houston in 1969 as one of the biggest breaks of my life! There virtually was no FM and the station was HOT!!! We released several albums in which they put pictures of their announcers inside the jackets. That's me on the far right (top) and just above the work "Rock" on the second album (bottom). The other announcers included from left to right, the original Hudson and Harrigan who have become legends. They were just plain funny and had the ratings to prove it. Bill Young was our program director and has this incredible voice and now his own production company. Rick Shaw with and without the beard was kind enough to teach me how to edit tape. John Michaels I consider a good friend and one of America's greatest announcers. In the first picture, Steve Lundy was Houston's most popular night announcer (very deep voiced dude).

In the second picture, Scotty Tripp took over that time slot. Scotty brought a whole new "attitude" to Houston radio . . . ahead of his time. Remind me or ask Debbie about our wild night with Scotty and his girl-friend in Hawaii. WoW! I'll never forget that ride. Walt "Baby" Love was a truly class act and was so highly rated at a competitive soul station that KILT hired him away to join the "Good Time 610 Men." Others, Jay Rogers, a guy we all thought was just super on the air, Johnny Shannon who was one of the best overnight announcers I have heard. These albums were popular for years. They sold hundreds of thousands of copies. I couldn't go anywhere without getting: "Don't I know you from somewhere"? Of course, I loved it.

My thanks to Mr. Rick Candea, current program director at KILT-AM/FM-the leading country station in Houston for being kind enough to mail these to me several Christmases ago. Also a special thanks to Mr. Dickie Rosenfeld who was the general manager at KILT before I got there in 1969 and is still the manager at this writing! He is a class act. And to all the guys I worked with . . . those were some great days and one great radio station! It was my honor to work with all of you.

(183) Q: **How were the bubbling sounds created in the two-time hit "Monster Mash"?**
A. *Someone blew a straw into a glass of water.*
B. *An underwater microphone was placed in Bobby "Boris" Pickett's fish tank.*
C. *A woman in a black hat got the effects from the beach.*
D. *The sounds were recorded in the back of a boat borrowed from Elvis Presley.*
Score: 5 points

(184) Q: **Which phrase uttered by Clark Gable in a movie became the foundation for a #1 song of 1962?**
A. *"Wishin' and Hopin'"*
B. *"Will You Still Love Me Tomorrow"?*
C. *"Big Girls Don't Cry"*
D. *"It's Now or Never"*
Score: 6 points

This is our son Chance's dog, Captain Hooch. 25 points if you can name this breed of dog. 10 seconds. Go! (Answer backwards: I am a EsenihC Gup).

(185) Q: **What do Frankie Tyler, Eric Anthony and Billy Dixon all have in common?**
A. *They were all movie names used at one time by Elvis.*
B. *They were all stage names used at one time by Franki Valli.*
C. *They were all at one time members of Danny and the Juniors.*
D. *They were the group 3 Dog Night.*
Score: 10 points

(186) Q: **What U.S. communications satellite became the title of a #1 record?**
A. *"Voyager I"*
B. *"Atlantis"*
C. *"Telstar"*
D. *"Hurricane"*
Score: 4 points

(187) Q: For the 27-week period that began on September 15, 1962, which group occupied the #1 position for an incredible 13 weeks!?
A. *The Beatles*
B. *The Four Seasons*
C. *The Supremes*
D. *The Shirelles*
Score: 10 points

(188) Q: Which #1 song of the rock era contains the spontaneous cry of "What Key? What Key"? from a rather confused musician?
A. *"Shout Part II"*
B. *"Honky Tonk Part II"*
C. *"Fingertips Part II"*
D. *"Hey Jude"*
Score: 5 points

(189) Q: Name the two most significant songs of the rock era.
A. *"Rock Around the Clock" and "I Wanna Hold Your Hand"*
B. *"Hound Dog" and "Suspicious Minds"*
C. *"The Twist" and "Moody Blue"*
D. *"Hound Dog" and "I Saw Her Standing There"*
Score: 10 points

(190) Q: Which group went to #1 in the U.S. first: the Byrds or the Rolling Stones?
Score: 5 points

Food Fight!!!

(191) Q: **How old was Brian Wilson when his parents noticed that he was singing . . . on key?**
A. 10
B. 9
C. 8
D. 3
Score: 6 points

(192) Q: **Who is Geno Sacco?**
A. *Franki Valli*
B. *Lou Christie*
C. *Gene Pitney*
D. *Ruby, of Ruby and the Romantics*
Score: 5 points

(193) Q: **What is the last name used in the "Name Game"?**
A. *Nick*
B. *Rick*
C. *Bob*
D. *Mary*
Score: 1 points

Judy Collins gives an unforgettable performance in 1969.

(194) Q: **How old was Paul Anka in 1990?**
A. *64*
B. *44*
C. *48*
D. *46*
Score: 6 points

(195) Q: **What famous solo artist of the sixties was a founding member of the Dovells?**
A. *Len Barry*
B. *Gene Pitney*
C. *Lou Christie*
D. *Robert Parker*
Score: 10 points

(196) Q: What is considered to be the first complete year in Rock 'N' Roll history?
A. 1955
B. 1956
C. 1957
D. 1958
Score: 4 points

(197) Q: How old was Sonny James when the classic "Young Love" hit the charts?
A. 34
B. 33
C. 29
D. 26
Score: 5 points

(198) Q: According to Zager and Evans, what will happen in the year 4545?
A. *They won't need their teeth.*
B. *They won't need their eyes.*
C. *Nobody will look at you.*
D. *We will be invaded by space aliens.*
Score: 10 points

"Hi! I'm Tonya Harding's boyfriend. Heh heh."

Page 55

Questions

"So are we!"

(199) Q: Which Beatle thought about leaving the group before the break-up but didn't "have the guts"?

A. John
B. Paul
C. George
D. Ringo
Score: 9 points

(200) Q: What did Dion do just before recording his hit "The Wanderer"?

A. *He had a few drinks.*
B. *He picked up his girlfriend(s) to watch him record the song.*
C. *He fasted for 3 days.*
D. *He bought a good luck charm from a gypsy.*
Score: 10 points

(201) Q: Besides James Dean, who else influenced Elvis's screen performance?

A. *Trick question—only James Dean*
B. *Dean Martin*
C. *Marlon Brando*
D. *Oliver Hardy*
Score: 4 points

(202) Q: Name the first Beatle song to utilize a four track studio.

A. *"I Wanna Hold Your Hand"*
B. *"She Loves You"*
C. *"All My Lovin'"*
D. *"Please Please Me"*
Score: 10 points

"Let's rock this joint!"

(203) Q: True or False? Elvis claimed to have a Bible in every room of his home in Graceland?

Score: 5 points

(204) **Q: What percentage of all single records sold in February 1964 is credited to the Beatles?**
A. Almost 10%
B. 30%
C. 50%
D. 60%
Score: 9 points

(205) **Q: What was the first girl group to tour with the Beatles?**
A. *Martha and the Vandellas*
B. *The Chiffons*
C. *The Supremes*
D. *The Sweet Inspirations*
Score: 9 points

(206) **Q: What famous sixties group said that they sang about "freedom, only we used another word for it"?**
A. *The Rascals*
B. *The Beach Boys*
C. *The Turtles*
D. *The O'Jays*
Score: 5 points

Tom Moffatt with the Everly Brothers, known for "Bye Bye Love", and "All I Have To Do Is Dream".

Questions

(207) **Q: Which Righteous Brothers' hit was panned by the critics as sounding as if it were playing at the wrong speed?**
A. *"Soul and Inspiration"*
B. *"Unchained Melody"*
C. *"You've Lost That Lovin' Feelin'"*
D. *All of the above*
Score: 5 points

(208) **Q: To whom did the Beatles dedicate their movie "Help"?**
A. *Brian Epstein*
B. *Marcus Welby*
C. *Elvis*
D. *Elias Howe*
Score: 9 points

(209)   Q: **Where did Sam the Sham get the idea for the song "Wolly Bully"?**

A. *He was making fun of Burt Reynolds' toupee.*
B. *That was his cat's name.*
C. *The name comes from an old African chant in which the "Wooly Bully" is actually an angry goat which rampages throughout the villages plundering the small thatched huts and "disturbing life for the tribe".*
D. *The name comes from a Brillo pad box.*
Score: 10 points

The sum of the squares of the sides of a triangle are equal to the square of its hypotenuse. Good grief!!!

(210)   Q: **What famous soul singer of the sixties was once a member of the "You're So Fine" Falcons?**

A. *James Brown*
B. *Wilson Pickett*
C. *Jackie Wilson*
D. *Otis Redding*
Score: 10 points

(211)   Q: **Who was/were the first American(s) to recognize the potential of the Beatles?**

A. *Elvis*
B. *The Sir Douglas Quintet*
C. *Ed Sullivan*
D. *Del Shannon*
Score: 10 points

(212) Q: Where did the Searchers get the idea for their name?
A. They had been searching for a name to use for over 3 months when it was decided that the fact that they had been searching would be a good idea . . . thus, the Searchers.
B. It was taken from a John Wayne movie.
C. John Lennon has suggested it as a name that the Beatles had at one time considered.
D. It was named after Search, England.
Score: 10 points

(213) Q: For his 34th birthday, Paul McCartney paid $600 to a comedian to entertain. Who?
A. John Belushi-doing Joe Cocker
B. Dick Van Dyke-doing Stan Laurel
C. Steve Martin-doing "Excuuuse me."
Score: 8 points

(214) Q: Which Beatle visited Elvis backstage when he performed in Las Vegas in the 1970s?
A. John
B. Paul
C. George
D. Ringo
Score: 9 points

From Left to Right: John, Paul, George and Ringo" (Just Kidding)

(215) Q: **Which Ricky Nelson song was originally written for Sam Cooke but turned down by Sam's manager?**
A. *"Hello Mary Lou"*
B. *"Garden Party"*
C. *"Travelin' Man"*
D. *"It's A Young World"*
Score: 10 points

(216) Q: **Who played guitar on many of the early Chuck Berry sessions?**
A. *15 year old Lonnie Mack*
B. *Bo Diddley*
C. *Glen Campbell*
D. *Chuck played all the guitar on every one of his recordings.*
Score: 10 points

Questions

(217) Q: **What does Mr. Green keep in every room in "Pleasant Valley Sunday"?**
A. *His make up*
B. *A shotgun*
C. *A television*
D. *A monkey*
Score: 7 points

(218) Q: **What type of guitar did Jimi Hendrix use?**
A. *A specially designed Octograph*
B. *A Les Paul*
C. *A special guitar designed by Chet Atkins*
D. *A Fender Stratocaster*
Score: 10 points

(219) Q: **Who produced Elvis's "Heartbreak Hotel"?**
A. *Mabel Axton*
B. *Hoyt Axton*
C. *Colonel Parker*
D. *Chet Atkins*
Score: 5 points

Now you can protect precious lives with

An all-concrete blast-resistant house

Here's a house with all the advantages of any concrete home—PLUS protection from atomic blasts at minimum cost.

A firesafe, attractive, *low-annual-cost* house, it provides comfortable living—PLUS a refuge for your family in this atomic age.

The blast-resistant house design is based on principles learned at Hiroshima and Nagasaki and at Eniwotok and Yucca Flats. It has a reinforced concrete first floor and roof and reinforced concrete masonry walls. The walls, the floor and the roof are tied together securely with reinforcement to form a rigidly integrated house that the engineers calculate will resist blast pressures 40% closer to bursts than conventionally-built houses.

Anywhere in the concrete basement of the house would be much safer than above ground but a special shelter area has been provided in this basement to protect occupants from blast pressures expected at distances as close as 3,600 feet from ground zero of a bomb with an explosive force equivalent to 20,000 tons of TNT. This shelter area affords protection from radiation, fire and flying debris as well. And the same shelter area also can serve as a refuge from the lesser violence of tornadoes, hurricanes and earthquakes.

The safety features built into this blast-resistant house are estimated by the architect and engineer to raise the cost less than 10%.

Concrete always has been known for its remarkable strength and durability. That's why it can be used economically to build houses with a high degree of safety from atomic blasts.

Like all concrete structures, blast-resistant concrete houses are moderate in first cost, require little maintenance and give long years of service. The result is *low-annual-cost* shelter. Write for folder.

(220) Q: **What was the flip side of the original print of the Everly Brothers' "All I Have To Do Is Dream," and who wrote it?**
A. *"Bye Bye Love" written by Don Everly*
B. *"Claudette" written by Phil Everly*
C. *Wake Up Little Susie" by Roy Orbison*
D. *"Claudette" by Roy Orbison*
Score: 3 points

(221) Q: **What was the original working title of the Beatles' "Let It Be" album?**
A. *"Let Me Be"*
B. *"Let Us Be"*
C. *"Let It Be"*
D. *"Get Back"*
Score: 6 points

(222) Q: **What famous singer of the sixties helped write many of the Four Seasons' hits?**
A. *Sonny Bono*
B. *Franki Valli*
C. *Gene Pitney*
D. *David Gates*
Score: 8 points

PURE GOLD ROCK 'N' ROLL TRIVIA

Questions

One of the voices heard nationwide on the Ron Foster show and the world's greatest sax player - Heather Huber.

Amid drums and amplifiers, The Tracers, back-up band for the English singing group THEM, entertain in the Main Ballroom.

(223) **Q: What do the TV "Gong Show" and the hit "Palisades Park" have in common?**
A. *They were both produced by Phil Spector.*
B. *They were both produced by Chet Atkins.*
C. *Chuck Barris hosted one and wrote the other.*
D. *They both debuted on the same day.*
Score: 7 points

(224) **Q: Who wrote Manfred Mann's big 1968 hit "The Mighty Quinn"?**
A. *Elton John*
B. *Manfred Mann*
C. *David Gates*
D. *Bob Dylan*
Score: 10 points

(225) **Q: What was the complete name of the Woodstock Festival?**
A. *The Woodstock Arts and Crafts Bazaar*
B. *The Woodstock Festival*
C. *The Woodstock Renaissance Festival and Craft Show*
D. *The Woodstock Music and Art Fair*
Score: 7 points

(226) **Q: How long did Buddy Holly's career last?**
A. *2 years*
B. *1 year*
C. *18 months*
D. *11 months*
Score: 7 points

(227) **Q: What was the flip side of Chuck Berry's first hit "Maybelline"?**
A. *"My Girl Josephine"*
B. *"Wee Wee Hours"*
C. *"Kid Prom"*
D. *"My Senior Prom"*
Score: 8 points

(228) **Q: Which Beach Boy sang lead on "Good Vibrations"?**
A. *Carl Wilson*
B. *Dennis Wilson*
C. *Brian Wilson*
D. *Jan of Jan and Dean*
Score: 9 points

(229) **Q: What was the Who's first U.S. hit?**
A. *"Magic Bus"*
B. *"I Can See Clearly Now"*
C. *"Happy Jack"*
D. *"Won't Get Fooled Again"*
Score: 7 points

(230) **Q: On which Beatle album cover(s) did all four sport mustaches?**
A. *"Sgt. Pepper"*
B. *"Meet the Beatles"*
C. *"Abbey Road" and "Sgt. Pepper"*
D. *"Sgt. Pepper" and "Let It Be"*
Score: 3 points

Remember when <u>all</u> the girls got tall at once?

(231) Q: In 1956 Columbia Records held a talent contest to find "another" Elvis Presley. The winner received a recording contract and actually got a hit record out of the deal. Who won?
A. Carl Perkins
B. Johnny Burnette
C. Gene Vincent
D. Eddie Cochran
Score: 10 points

BONUS TIME

Three questions each worth 25 points. Are you ready? You will have 10 seconds on each question. These questions are not multiple choice. Ready? Here we go.

(232) Q: Jimmy Swaggart and Mickey Gilley have a famous cousin. Who? 10-9-8-7-6-5-4-3-2-1. BINGO

(233) Q: Debbie Reynolds had one hit. Name it. 10-9-8-7-6-5-4-3-2-1. BINGO

(234) Q. Ann Margaret had one hit. Name it. 10-9-8-7-6-5-4-3-2-1. BINGO

Wanna tie one on?

Questions

(235) Q: Who had the original version of "A Thousand Stars"?
A. Kathy Young
B. The Innocents
C. The Rivileers
D. The Rivilettes
Score: 10 points

Bonus Time!
Name all of these famous Actors for 10 points each.

Questions

Answers: Top Left: Bette Davis, Top Right: Bing Crosby, Bottom Left: Humphrey Bogart, Bottom Right: James Dean.

Debbie and her best friend Glenna in the old 25¢ picture booth. Now it's probably $10.00.

(236) **Q: What is the chord progression on "Turn On Your Lovelight" made famous by Bobby Bland?**
A. C, A minor, F, G
B. C, F, C, F, C, F, etc.
C. A, D, E, A, D, E
D. D, C, D, C, C, c
Score: 10 points unless you are a musician. If you are a musician you are only allowed 1 point. Sorry but those are the rules as decided by . . . Captain Hooch.

(237) **Q: Frankie Avalon and Bobby Rydell both belonged to what Philadelphia band in the fifties?**
A. The Nightliners
B. The Nightriders
C. Rocco and the Saints
D. Rocco and the Beats
Score: 10 points

(238) **Q: How much did Chuck Berry pay for his first guitar?**
A. It cost him nothing; it was made from cereal boxes.
B. It was made from popsicle sticks and cost nothing.
C. $4.00
D. $10.00
Score: 7 points

(239) **Q: What was the fateful flight number on "Ebony Eyes"?**
A. 1103
B. 1203
C. 121
D. 17
Score: 10 points

(240) Q: Paul Anka wrote and sang "Put Your Head on my Shoulder" and "Puppy Love" for what famous Mousekateer?
A. *Andrea Fineley*
B. *Annette Funicello*
C. *Brenda Lee*
D. *Shelley Fabares*
Score: 10 points (What the heck . . . they deserve a chance too)!

A big "Hi" from the "Future Lion tamers of America."

(241) Q: He has sold over 50 million records, placed more than 48 singles in the top 100 on the pop charts. He has hosted "Saturday Night Live" and duetted with Bob Dylan. He produced a movie about the life of Jesus Christ. Who is he?
A. *Pat Boone*
B. *Conway Twitty*
C. *Johnny Cash*
D. *Bob Dylan*
Score: 10 points

Armcross competition—Referee jabs contestants in the ear every 3 minutes to see who gives first.

(242) Q: Name the first #1 song of the Rock Era to be written by the same person who sang it.
A. *"Summertime Blues" by Eddie Cochran*
B. *"Party Doll" by Buddy Knox*
C. *"Pretty Woman" by Roy Orbison*
D. *"Only the Lonely" by Roy Orbison*
Score: 10 points

Page 68

PURE GOLD ROCK ROLL TRIVIA

Questions

(243) Q: Richie Valens had a hit with "Donna." Who wrote the song?
A. Richie Valens
B. Gene Pitney
C. Rudy Martinez
D. Gene Chandler
Score: 5 points

(244) Q: What famous actor had a 1957 hit with "Moonlight Swim" and has appeared in the movies as a woman?
A. Paul Simon
B. Tony Curtis
C. Jack Lemmon
D. Anthony Perkins
Score: 7 points

(245) Q: What was the Coaster's first hit?
A. "Charlie Brown"
B. "Searchin'"
C. "Yakety Yak"
D. "Smooth Sailin'"
Score: 8 points

(246) Q: What was the first Beatle song on which George Harrison played a 12 string guitar?
A. "Norweigan Wood"
B. "Michelle"
C. "Girl"
D. "You Can't Do That"
Score: 10 points

Questions

Just makes ya' hungry, don't it?

(247) True or false? Dick Clark once said that the Colonel: " . . . kept Elvis in a cage like an animal . . . and (he) trotted him out like a caged bear."
Score: 10 points

(248) True or false? Between 1961 and 1969 Elvis performed no live shows.
Score: 10 points

(249) True or false? Elvis was known to wear lifts in his shoes and boots to look taller?
Score: 10 points

(250) True or false? Elvis once gave Jack Lord of "Hawaii Five-O" a pair of matching Berrettas. Lord gave Elvis a rare six-string banjo in return for the favor?
Score: 10 points

(251) True or false? When Elvis died his estate was estimated to be around five million dollars.
Score: 10 points

(252) True or false? Lisa Marie reportedly became a member of the Scientology sect. Other members reportedly include John Travolta and Sonny Bono.
Score: 10 points

(253) True or false? Lisa Marie was born exactly nine months after Elvis and Pricilla were married?
Score: 10 points

(254) True or false? Lisa Marie's middle name was selected as an honor to Colonel Parker's wife, Marie?
Score: 10 points

(255) True or false? When Elvis met Pricilla for the first time she was wearing a blue-and-white sailor suit dress with white socks?
Score: 10 points

ONE OF THE KING'S FINAL CONCERTS . . .

Questions

The irony of ironies is that Elvis was a virtual prisoner due to his popularity yet he loved people. The only time Elvis could really "touch" the public he loved was when he was doing the very thing that was causing his inability to be seen in public.

(256)　True or false? In 1948 Gladys Presley was working as a nurse's aide at $4.00 a day.
Score: 10 points

(257)　True or false? After Gladys Presley's death, Vernon, Elvis's dad remarried a blue-eyed Davada "Dee" Stanley. Elvis did not attend the wedding.
Score: 10 points

(258)　True or false? Vernon was an 8th grade dropout when he married Gladys Love Smith?
Score: 10 points

(259)　True or false? Gladys was four years older than Vernon?
Score: 10 points

(260)　True or false? Vernon served nine months at Mississippi's Parchman Penitentiary on a conviction of forgery when Elvis was still a toddler.
Score: 10 points

(261)　True or false? Eighteen of Elvis's more than 650 songs reached the top of the charts.
Score: 10 points

(262)　True or false? Elvis was the first artist to sell a million copies of a pop record.
Score: 10 points

(263)　True or false? Tommy Durden, a retired dishwasher repairman co-wrote "Heartbreak Hotel" with Mae Boren Axton.
Score: 10 points

(264)　True or false? Elvis recorded at least seven songs containing the word "blue."
Score: 10 points

(265)　True or false? Elvis would often make travel reservations under the name "Dr. John Carpenter."
Score: 10 points

A BITTERSWEET GLIMPSE OF THE KING

This never-before-released photo of Elvis somehow seems to capture both The King's youth and his final days. The shot was taken during a final Vegas performance and stands alone as one of the classic Elvis shots.

(266) True or false? Elvis would often make travel reservations under the name "John Burrows" or "Colonel John Burrows."
Score: 10 points

(267) True or false? "All Shook Up" was written by Otis Blackwell and was inspired when he was sitting in the offices of Shalimar Music and one of the owners shook a bottle of Pepsi and challenged Blackwell to write a song about it. It was one of Elvis's biggest hits, spending a total of 30 weeks on the charts.
Score: 10 points

(268) True or false? Elvis studied numerology, the occult, metaphysics and the New Age; he also read about UFOs and often talked about reincarnation.
Score: 10 points

(269) True or false? At one time Elvis travelled with Scatter, a frisky chimpanzee who was known to dress in shirt and trousers and hold a whisky glass and pound it on a bar until someone filled it.
Score: 10 points

(270) True or false? At one time Elvis owned a Pyrenean mountain dog named Muffin who once chased Elvis and Pricilla into Graceland nearly biting the King.
Score: 10 points

(271) True or false? Elvis hated being called "E" or "El" and particularly disliked the name "Elvis the Pelvis" which he said was "stupid."
Score: 10 points

(272) True or false? Gladys Presley was uncomfortable with Elvis's fame and worried that she was too heavy and unsophisticated.
Score: 10 points

(273) True or false? Elvis was 22 when he bought Graceland.
Score: 10 points

THE KING . . .

Picture taken months before we lost The King of rock 'n' roll.

"Now, on with the hits!"

(274) **Q: What was Peter, Paul and Mary's biggest hit?**
A. *"Leavin' On A Jet Plane"*
B. *"Puff The Magic Dragon"*
C. *"Blowin' in the Wind"*
D. *"I Dig Rock and Roll Music"*
Score: 5 points

(275) **Q: What was the very first song Ricky Nelson recorded?**
A. *"Travelin' Man"*
B. *"Poor Little Fool"*
C. *"Blueberry Hill"*
D. *"I'm Walkin'"*
Score: 7 points

(276) **Q: What was Debbie Reynold's highest charted song?**
A. *"Tammy" was credited to Debbie Reynolds, but the voice was dubbed in by a 12 year old Andy Williams.*
B. *"Banana Boat" with her husband Eddie Fisher*
C. *"Tammy"–she sang the song*
D. *"Across the Sea"*
Score: 4 points

(277) **Q: What was Buddy Holly's real name?**
A. *Hardin "Bubba" Holly*
B. *Charles Hardin Holley*
C. *Buddy Edward Holly*
D. *Edmund "Bubba" Holly*
Score: 8 points

(278) **Q: On the back of whose album were these kind words written? "Greetings . . . to the swingin'est of all swingin' yon Teen-Agers, (and all the young at heart), in this here nation. Here is the bootin' album that you have asked for by _____. Dig the smash sound of _____ and the Socko _____ and the Rockin' _____. . . . Plus 9 of the gassiest golden groovies any red-blooded music lover would want . . . "?**
A. *Conway Twitty*
B. *Buddy Holly*
C. *The Coasters*
D. *The Four Seasons*
Score: 10 points

(278) Q: How long did it take the Beatles to record their first album?
A. *12 hours*
B. *12 days*
C. *Two weeks*
D. *6 weeks*
Score: 9 points

(279) Q: What was Chuck Berry's first hit?
A. *"Johnny B. Goode"*
B. *"Too Much Monkey Business"*
C. *"Rock and Roll Music"*
D. *"Maybellene"*
Score: 4 points

(280) Q: What country was the popular group the "Sir Douglas Quintet" from?
A. *America*
B. *Australia*
C. *England*
D. *Scotland*
Score: 8 points

(281) Q: What unusual thing happened during the recording of "Heartbreak Hotel"?
A. *Three year old Hoyt Axton who was attending the session with his mother, who wrote the song, and began to cry during the actual recording. The Axtons were eventually asked to leave by the Colonel, but Elvis insisted they stay.*
B. *Elvis split his pants.*
C. *Jerry Lee Lewis dropped a nickel in the soda machine, the noise came through on the recording and the session had to be redone.*
D. *Elvis attempted his first karate kick on the Colonel after Parker demanded more money*
Score: 4 points

(282) **Q: Who co-wrote "Maybe Baby" with Buddy Holly but was not credited on the label?**
A. *The Bib Bopper*
B. *George Jones*
C. *Buddy's mom*
D. *Richie Valens*
Score: 4 points

(283) **Q: During "Elvis's first and only news conference" in 1972, what did the King say was the reason he had outlasted all of the rock stars of the fifties and sixties?**
A. *Elvis gave the credit to the Colonel.*
B. *His mother*
C. *Vitamin E*
D. *His wife Pricilla got the credit.*
Score: 9 points

(284) **Q: What do Glen Campbell, Perry Como and Johnny Rivers have in common?**
A. *The same birthday*
B. *The same religious faith*
C. *They all had 6 children.*
D. *They are all 7th sons of 7th sons.*
Score: 10 points

(285) **Q: What was the last album recorded by the Beatles?**
A. *"Abbey Road"*
B. *"The Long and Winding Road"*
C. *"Let It Be"*
D. *"Sgt. Pepper"*
Score: 2 points

(286) **Q: Who had the original version of Pat Boone's "I Almost My Mind"?**
A. *Who else? Little Richard*
B. *The Big Bopper*
C. *Larry Williams*
D. *Ivory Joe Hunter*
Score: 4 points

Off to the drive-in!

(287)   Q: What did
         "Little Egypt"
         have in her
         tummy?
         A. A bell
         B. A bone
         C. A diamond
         D. A ruby
         Score: 7 points

(288)   Q: In the fifties,
         Jerry Butler was
         the leader for
         what group?
         A. The Miracles
         B. The Drifters
         C. The Impressions
         D. The Imperials
         Score: 8 points

Debbie plants one on Mr. Bob Hope. Thanks for the memories.

Questions

(289)   Q: What has Paul of Paul and Paula been doing
         since "Hey Paula" was a hit?
         A. Paul has owned and managed a jazz club in New Orleans.
         B. Paul retired just after "Hey Paula" sold a million copies.
         C. Paul owns a small club in Honolulu, Hawaii and is a minis-
         ter to the native islanders during the day.
         D. Paul has been a volunteer with the Fellowship of Christian
         Athletes.
         Score: 7 points

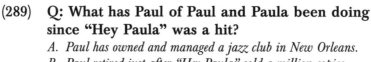

(290)   Q: What quirk of fate cost Aretha Franklin "millions and millions"
         of dollars, kept her from mounting a full-fledged concert tour and
         kept her from a lead role in a musical biography of Mahalia
         Jackson?
         A. Aretha was on several very shaky airplane flights and was afraid to fly.
         B. Aretha was almost hit by lightning while performing outdoors in New Orleans and
         since that day has refused to travel.
         C. Aretha Franklin has suffered from extreme stage fright since her father forced her to
         sing in front of a church as a child.
         D. Aretha would rather spend the time with her family considering that her childhood
         was as an only child.
         Score: 6 points

(291)   Q: Name the first white act to be signed to Motown?
A. *Danny and the Juniors*
B. *Dion and the Belmonts*
C. *Rare Earth*
D. *America*
Score: 10 points

(292)   Q: Over the years how many musical acts have appeared on "American Bandstand"?
A. *Over 25,000*
B. *Over 10,000*
C. *About 9,000*
D. *About 5,000*
Score: 10 points

(293)   Q: Which female artist of the rock era has taken home the most Grammys?
A. *Diana Ross*
B. *Connie Francis*
C. *Aretha Franklin*
D. *Cher*
Score: 9 points

(294)   Q: Which popular fifties group was Wilson Pickett once a member of?
A. *The Impressions*
B. *The Impalas*
C. *The Fiestas*
D. *The Falcons*
Score: 4 points

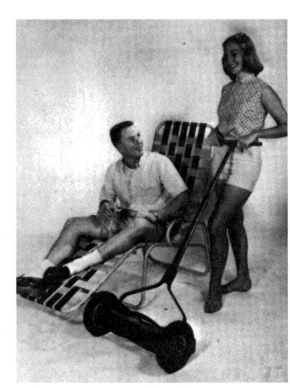

After the 1950's, men did the mowing. (Let's not mention power mowers that pull themselves).

(295)   Q: What was NBC's response to the popularity of "Shindig"?
A. *They counter programmed with "Batman".*
B. *They ran "American Bandstand" reruns against it.*
C. *They concocted "The Glen Campbell Goodtime Hour".*
D. *They countered with "Hullabaloo.".*
Score: 9 points

(296) Q: Which Beatle song was about a weekend hippie?
A. "Hey Jude"
B. "Day Tripper"
C. "Rocky Racoon"
D. "Lucy in the Sky"
Score: 7 points

(297) Q: The Rolling Stones have a reputation for being a little rough on hotel suites while they are on tour. What does Mick Jagger blame this on?
A. The bad food.
B. They get nervous on tour with all the girls crowding around them and "take it out on the room".
C. They go crazy.
D. The flights bother them.
Score: 8 points

Questions

(298) True or false? Franki Valli once worked as a gardener for Natalie Wood before becoming a singing star.
Score: 5 points

(299) True or false? Franki Valli worked in a country band when he was 15 by faking the upright bass.
Score: 5 points

(300) Q: Frankie Valli and the Four Seasons were not a successful group until they began to emulate what other famous act?
A. The Beach boys
B. The Four Tops
C. Maurice Williams and the Zodiacs
D. The Everly Brothers
Score: 8 points

(301) Q: Where did the group Cream get their name?

A. *They were on tour in England as the "Gollywods" when a waiter brought them a tray of desserts. He said: "These are better with cream . . ." and the rest, as they say, is history.*

B. *On their own assumption that they were the "cream of the crop" of the British invasion*

C. *The tour bus they were on got hit by a truck. No one was hurt, but the driver of the truck yelled: "Hey, you guys have been creamed!" They were so elated that they really were not injured that they took this as Divine Intervention.*

D. *None of the above*

Score: 10 points

"*. . . and so, in conclusion, I think real men should not wear silly sissy deodorant. A man should smell like a man.*"

Questions

(302) Q: Who was the only soul singer to show up at the Monterey Pop Festival?

A. *Jimi Hendrix*

B. *Otis Redding*

C. *Wilson Pickett*

D. *James Brown*

Score: 6 points

(303) Q: Creedance Clearwater Revival's Swampland vocals give away their heritage, but what part of the state are they from?

A. *They are all New Orleans natives.*

B. *They are from Baton Rouge.*

C. *CCR actually originated in Texas.*

D. *They are from Northern California.*

Score: 7 points

(304) **Q: About how many records did the Beatles sell by 1970?**
A. *Almost 22 million*
B. *Just under 40 million*
C. *Over 200 million*
D. *Over 500 million*
Score: 9 points

(305) **Q: B.J. Thomas had allegedly been a substance addict since age 15 and estimated that he had spent between two and three million dollars on drugs by the mid seventies. How did he quit?**
A. *On January 28, 1978 B.J. entered a rehabilitation home.*
B. *B.J. was helped by his close friend, Robert Redford, on the set of "Butch Cassidy and the Sundance Kid".*
C. *B.J. became a born again Christian.*
D. *B.J. could simply no longer afford the drugs.*
Score: 10 points

(306) **Q: Where did the Four Seasons invite Sherry?**
A. *To the hop*
B. *To a twist party*
C. *To a toga party*
D. *For a ride*
Score: 6 points

"Today, I am going to discuss the effects of too much hair spray."

(307) **True or false? Tommy Sands was once married to Nancy Sinatra.**
Score: 5 points

(308) **True or false? Johnny Crawford, Paul Peterson and Annette Funicello were all members of the Mouseketeers.**
Score: 5 points

(309) Q: How did Simon and Garfunkle achieve the "explosion" sound on their hit "Bridge Over Troubled Waters"?

A. *They slammed an expensive baby grand piano shut.*
B. *The crash came from a door closing-the effect was slowed down and the volume turned up to create the effect.*
C. *The so called crashing sound is actually an amplifier falling over. The "crash" was left on the track for effect.*
D. *The effect was achieved by kicking an amplifier which was turned up all the way, slowing the sound, and whispering "Whaaaa" in the background.*

Score: 10 points

(310) Q: He met Pat Boone at North Texas State University where he was inspired by Pat to enter the recording industry. Who is he?

A. *Bob Dylan*
B. *Wayne Newton*
C. *B.J. Thomas*
D. *Roy Orbison*

Score: 8 points

Questions

Tom Moffatt with the original Platters

BEHIND THE SCENES . . . BEATLES!

Coliseum, Houston, Texas, 1965. I had managed to get inside with a little mini-tape recorder. (Try doing that at a concert these days . . . on second thought . . . don't). The Beatles! And we had 50th row tickets! Wow, was this gonna be great!!!

The crowd was intense. You didn't smell pot in the air. There was no head banging, just a lot of screams everytime anyone who even looked like a Beatle walked toward the stage.

The lights dimmed.

The girls screamed.

A comedian came on. I remember thinking: "This is dumb. A comedian? You gotta be kidding." The guy may have been okay because a lot of laughs were heard, mostly anticipatory, anxious laughs . . . the kind of nervous laugh you throw at your boss when he tells a lousy joke. The guy finished.

The lights dimmed again. More screams. Some announcer tried to be heard over the noise. Suddenly, there they were! The Beatles! I rolled tape.

The first thing that struck me was their size; these guys appeared short . . . couldn't have been over 5'8" . . . at least that's the way it looked. They seemed to be enjoying the reception, but they appeared a little nervous and almost like they were going through the motions. What they

The following three photos were taken on the Beatles' first tour of the U.S. (1965) in Miami, Florida, in a hotel elevator. Much thanks to Terrie Johnson for the use of these never before published photographs.

sounded like didn't matter . . . all you could hear was one loud "waaaaaaa." We stood up on our chairs and, as only I could manage . . . I fell to the ground and got tangled under the seats! Good grief.

No one heard me. How could they? The Beatles were on stage! I remember feeling a tinge of panic as . . . there I was . . . stuck on the floor under the chairs . . . and nobody cared. Talk about humility. I wasn't hurt; I just couldn't get off the ground for a few minutes.

The concert in a word: Screaming. I heard maybe one or two notes. All I got on tape was the "Waaaaaaaa."

The Beatles created their own momentum at their press conference. They were different than anything that had come before them in rock and roll. This whole trip seemed to them like a game they were playing, enjoying and winning. They represented not so much a "new" music as a new outlook on life.

Looking back I see two sets of Beatles: the early Beatles with songs like "You think you've lost your love? Well, I saw her yesterday. It's you she's thinking of and she told me what to say. She said she loves you."

And, I see the Beatles after the gurus and the drugs. With words that didn't make sense forwards or backwards. Music that lost its vitality . . . its fun.

The early Beatles were exciting . . . funny . . . unique . . . a shot in the rock 'n' roll arm. Those are the four guys from Liverpool that impressed me.

Questions

THE BEATLES

Many thanks to Terri Johnson for the use of these never before published photographs of The Beatles.

(311) **Q: Which of these songs was released only after the group begged the producers to shelf it? They were embarrassed by the song!**
A. *"Make It With You"*
B. *"The Lion Sleeps Tonight"*
C. *"Surfin' Bird"*
D. *"Only the Lonely"*
Score: 10 points

(312) **Q: Who has been called the "most successful unknown in show business"?**
A. *Tiny Tim*
B. *Bobby Vinton*
C. *Tommy Lee Sturgeoun*
D. *Johnny Rivers*
Score: 10 points

The Heart Breakers.

(313) **Q: What was the significance of TWA flight 101 which landed at New York's Kennedy Airport in 1964?**
A. *The Beatles got off the plane and the British invasion was launched.*
B. *The Rolling Stones departed, ready to make their American debut. In just three weeks they would be outselling the Beatles.*
C. *Elvis Presley left for Honolulu for his "Satellite" comeback special broadcast. This program, more than any other, put Elvis back on the charts.*
D. *The Beatles got on board this plane to leave for England after a disastrous meeting with American record labels.*
Score: 6 points

(314) **Q: Of the following, who set a conference record of 6' 5 1/2" for the high jump at San Francisco State College?**
A. *Johnny Mathis*
B. *Johnny Rivers*
C. *Rick Nelson*
D. *John Denver*
Score: 7 points

(315) Q: "Surfin' U.S.A." by the Beach Boys was based on what famous song's melody?
A. "Fun, Fun, Fun"
B. "Johnny B. Goode"
C. "Sweet Little 16"
D. "Bony Moronie"
Score: 8 points

(316) Q: What kind of food does "Alley Oop" eat?
A. *Beer crate brew*
B. *Bear stew*
C. *Bearcat brew*
D. *Bearcat stew*
Score: 4 points

Ron Foster and Bruce Johnston. Bruce replaced Brian Wilson of the Beach Boys and is one of the very nicest people you could ever want to meet. Keep cookin' Bruce!

Page 90

Questions

(317) Q: What was the Everly Brothers' biggest hit in the U.S.?
A. *"Wake Up Little Susie"*
B. *"Bye Bye Love"*
C. *"All I Have to Do is Dream"*
D. *"Cathy's Clown"*
Score: 9 points

(318) Q: Who is generally credited with discovering Wayne Newton?
A. *Johnny Carson*
B. *Roy Orbison*
C. *Neil Sedaka*
D. *Bobby Darin*
Score: 10 points

(319) Q: Name the first artist(s) to record for the Motown label.
A. *Smokey Robinson*
B. *Jackie Wilson*
C. *Mary Wells*
D. *The Temptations*
Score: 9 points

(320) **True or False? The musicians were so impressed with the high note that Roy Orbison hit at the end of "Running Scared" that they stopped playing.**
Score: 9 points

(321) **Q: What do "Da Doo Ron Ron" and "Do Wah Diddy Diddy" have in common?**
A. They both reached #1 on the same day.
B. They were both written by Gene Pitney.
C. They were both written by the same duo.
D. They were both exactly 2:20 seconds long and released on the same day.
Score: 8 points

(322) **Q: What was the Dave Clark Fives' only #1 single?**
A. Captain Trivia . . . you don't fool me . . . this is a trick question
B. "Because"
C. "Over and Over"
D. "Catch Us If You Can"
Score: 10 points

(323) **Q: What was Elvis's favorite Elvis song?**
A. "It's Now or Never"
B. "Love Me Tender"
C. "Can't Help Falling In Love"
D. "Don't"
Score: 5 or 10 points

Ron Foster, Debbie Foster, and one of my best bubbas, Kerby Anderson and his lovely wife Susanne. No, Kerby is not a geek! We were going to a '50's party and that was the way he was supposed to look.

(324) **Q: Which Lou Christie song featured Linda Scott of "I Told Every Little Star" fame on vocals with Lou?**
A. *"Rhapsody In the Rain"*
B. *"I'm Gonna Make You Mine"*
C. *"Lightning Strikes"*
D. *Linda Scott never sang with Lou Christie. This is another trick question.*
Score: 10 points

(325) **Q: What Neil Diamond song did the Monkees take to #1?**
A. *"Last Train to Clarksville"*
B. *"Vallerie"*
C. *"I'm a Believer"*
D. *"Hey Hey We're the Monkees"*
Score: 5 points

(326) **Q: What #1 song of 1966 was based on the fact that "dogs bark at some people but not at others"?**
A. *"Shaggey Dog"*
B. *"Walkin' the Dog"*
C. *"I'll Be Doggoned"*
D. *"Good Vibrations"*
Score: 5 points

Questions

"Ham goes in this end . . . and presto . . . Spam!"

(327) **Q: When "Cherish" by The Association was #1 the week of September 24, 1966, what song was #2?**
A. *"96 Tears"*
B. *"Hurdy Gurdy Man"*
C. *"You Can't Hurry Love"*
D. *"See You in September"*
Score: 10 points–who remembers who came in at #2?

(328) **Q: What two artists were nicknamed the "Nurk Twins"?**
A. *Simon and Garfunkle*
B. *Phil and Don the Everly Brothers*
C. *John and Paul*
D. *Sam and Dave*
Score: 5 points

(329) **Q: What was the final #1 instrumental of the fifties?**
A. *"Sleepwalk"*
B. *"Last Night"*
C. *"Wild Weekend"*
D. *"Wipe Out"*
Score: 10 points

"Hold onto your hat."

(330) **Q: Who said: "Christianity will go. It will vanish and shrink. I needn't argue about that. I'm right and I'll be proved right . . . "**
A. *John Lennon*
B. *George Harrison*
C. *Elton John*
D. *Brenda Lee*
Score: 1 point

(331) **Q: How many harmony voices besides those of Simon and Garfunkle are heard on "Mrs. Robinson"?**
A. *2-Sonny and Cher*
B. *1-Bob Dylan*
C. *3-John, Paul and George*
D. *0-the four part harmony was Simon and Garfunkle singing with themselves.*
Score: 7 points

THE NIGHT I MET THE BEACH BOYS

It was 1964 and the Beach Boys were playing the Music Hall in Houston, Texas. I was the lead singer for a hot local group called the Detours. A group called the Dynamics was the opening act for the Beach Boys. Now, catch this! The Detours bought our jackets from the Dominos who had a local hit with "Shout" and the Dynamics were borrowing their jackets. Follow me? The Dynamics were borrowing the Detours jackets we had bought from the Dominos. They were red dress jackets with a "D" on the pocket and a black note through it. Cornball I know, but it was 1964 so give the kid a break. Here's the good part. There were four Dynamics and six Detours. Two jackets not being used by the Dynamics who were the opening act . . . hmmmm.

My friend and I showed up at the back door of the Music Hall with the jackets which didn't fit . . . and our guitar cases which were empty. The secu-

rity officer wasn't about to let us in even though I was pretty convincing as a "backup singer for the Dynamics . . . really man!" It didn't work. No one could get within a mile of that concert without a ticket. Everybody was trying every scam they could come up with. The Beach Boys were hot! I just told the guard that if anything happened it was fine with me because I was

Mike Love of the Beach Boys and Ron Foster. During this outing I was able to ask Mike Love some serious Beach Boy trivia. He told me that he and Paul McCartney happened to be staying at the same hotel when he saw Paul coming into the lobby and singing the words to a song about the U.S.S.R. It was here that Mike suggested they include a little Beach Boys' flavor and include the names of the cities from which the girls in the song came similar to what the Beach Boys had done with "California Girls". Paul liked the idea and we got "Moscow girls, etc." on the Beatles' hit "Back In The U.S.S.R."

union . . . getting paid anyway . . . I got his badge number and we began to walk off.

Backstage was really neat! The Dynamics were on and cookin'! The girls were screaming. I think our group was actually hotter, but the Dynamics had this drummer with blue hair combed in Beatle style and that got all the screams. They were good. I was at the curtain just watching them when I noticed a somehow familiar face next to me. I knew it was a Beach Boy but I didn't know who. It was Dennis Wilson! Now, act cool. Don't lose it. He's just a guy like you. So, I just kept on watching the show and he went away.

A few minutes later I wandered to the very back of the stage and sat down at this old piano and began to pick out the one song I knew, "Blueberry Hill." The band playing onstage was so loud that I couldn't hear myself anyway. All of a sudden the piano seemed to come alive! I looked to my right and in that backstage darkness sitting next to me was Dennis Wilson!

"Blueberry Hill"? he asked.

"Yeah. Know it"?

"Sure."

Man, I couldn't believe it. It was like a dream. I was playing a piano duet with Dennis Wilson! Nobody at Texas City High School would believe this one. Dennis was quite talented on the piano as best I could hear. All of a sudden the party was over. Some security dude stood over us and told us we'd have to lay off the piano because it was being heard "between numbers."

"Yes sir." I put my hands at my side and smiled. So did Dennis. When the officer began to walk away, Dennis began to play. The officer looked back, looked stern, then smiled, shook his head and went away. I just watched Dennis play the piano and felt cool.

A few minutes later I somehow got the nerve to ask Dennis if my friend and I could go into the dressing room and meet the other guys and maybe they could teach us the chords to "Warmth of the Sun." The only Beach Boys' song we even attempted was "Barbara Ann" and we did a lousy job on that. He told me he'd be right back, went into the dressing room, and came out in about five minutes looking a little down. Dennis Wilson always seemed to be smiling. Until then. I didn't dare ask him anything but he sensed my question.

Questions

"I don't know," was the last thing he said to me. There was a tint of fear in his eyes. I wondered if he'd gotten into trouble.

The door opened. I looked into the dressing room. There they were . . . The Beach Boys!!! It was them! They were sitting on this old couch. The door closed. Drat! A few minutes went by. The door opened.

"Hey, I'm sorry but . . . " I think that was Carl.

"Oh, that's okay." I tried to force a smile.

Oh well. It was worth the trip. The door shut. There was something wrong in that room . . . I sensed it. What, I didn't know. It was like they wanted to be nice, but they maintained this kind of fake "distance" as if they really didn't want to.

"Hey!" It was a voice from the dressing room. "You guys can come on in."

There we were! In the Beach Boys dressing room! Yo! I explained who we were, that we loved their music, and I asked if they could maybe show us the chords to "Warmth of the Sun" because we were trying to learn it but couldn't. Someone handed me a 12 string guitar. It was the first time I had even seen one. Wow! In a second the Beach Boys were showing us the chords and harmony to the song! I saw Brian Wilson sitting a few feet away on the edge of the couch. He kind of forced a smile and looked away. After just a few moments I broke in.

"No way we can learn this. The chords are to hard."

"Nah man. You can get it . . . "

There was a knock at the door.

"You guys are on." It was one of their road crew indicating the show was on for them and over for us. I could hear the anticipatory screams already. We shook hands and they told us to come back and they would finish teaching us the song. I don't remember who said it. The next thing I knew, they were gone and I was watching the show. The same guys who had been so nice to us just a few moments ago were now being mobbed by girls as police formed lines in front of the stage.

I always wondered why they had seemed so "stand-off-ish" at first. There was something wrong but I couldn't put my finger on it.

It was almost 20 years later when the news came out. Brian Wilson had "flipped out" on the jet on the way to that concert. He had sat on that jet, put his head into a pillow, and just screamed. That very night in 1964 in

Houston, Texas was Brian's last concert tour and we had seen it! Even through all the pain . . . the Beach Boys were nice enough to let us feel "The Warmth of the Sun."

God bless you guys.

Top: When the Beach Boys were in town a couple of years ago, they were in the middle of a very busy schedule. Yet Al Jardine, one of the original Beach Boys was nice enough to pose for these pictures with me and Bottom: Shawna, Al, Debbie, Chance. He then took us inside the dressing room to meet the other Beach Boys. Thanks Al! And what a dynamite concert!

(332) **Q: Where was Archie Bell when "Tighten Up" went to #1?**
A. *Archie had given up on the song becoming a hit and had returned to his job at a car dealership as a mechanic.*
B. *He was in a German hospital recovering from a leg wound he suffered in Viet Nam.*
C. *He was in Hawaii auditioning for "Hawaii Five-O".*
D. *Archie was in Houston, Texas teaching dance lessons.*
Score: 8 points

(333) **Q: Who did Bobby Goldsboro tour with as a backup singer before having a hit of his own?**
A. *The Beatles*
B. *Elton John*
C. *Glen Campbell*
D. *Roy Orbison*
Score: 10 points

(334) **Q: Name the only American #1 single to originate in France.**
A. *"All You Need Is Love"*
B. *"Venus"*
C. *"Love is Blue"*
D. *"Quiet Village"*
Score: 9 points

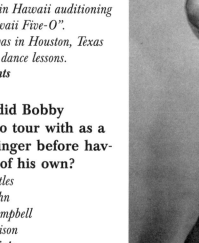

Trick or treat!

(334) **Q: What song, inspired by a Beatles' hit ironically knocked a Beatle song out of the #1 slot?**
A. *"Surf City"*
B. *"California Girls"*
C. *"Judy in Disguise"*
D. *"Devil in Disguise"*
Score: 9 points

(336) **Q: What was the 59th #1 song of the rock era which entered the charts at #59 and was the #2 song of '59?**

A. *"Little Darlin'"*
B. *"Mac the Knife"*
C. *"Last Date"*
D. *"Hurt So Bad"*
Score: 10 points

(337) **Q: About which American #1 hit did the British trade papers attack with the headline: "Blood Runs In The Grooves"?**

A. *"Patches"*
B. *"Tragedy"*
C. *"Dead Man's Curve"*
D. *"Teen Angel"*
Score: 10 points

(338) **Q: What was the Everly Brothers' most successful British hit?**

A. *The Everly Brothers never had a hit in England.*
B. *"Wake Up Little Susie"*
C. *"Cathy's Clown"*
D. *"Catch a Star" (A song not released in the U.S.)*
Score: 10 points

Questions

Left to right: Eric, Ashley, Chance, Travis. 5th grade. Before performing "Little Darlin" at Pope Elementary.

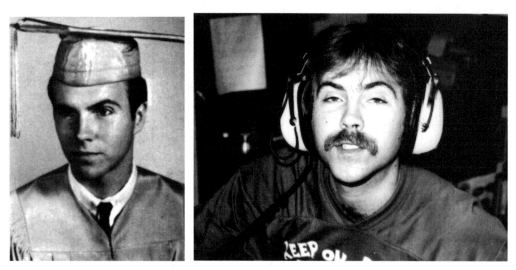

Captain Trivia . . . Before and after radio.

Questions

(339) **Q: What was Elvis's biggest selling single?**
A. *"Hound Dog"*
B. *"It's Now or Never"*
C. *"Suspicious Minds"*
D. *"Are You Lonesome Tonight"?*
Score: 8 points

(340) **Q: What #1 hit came from the "Donna Reed Show"?**
A. *"Johnny Angel"*
B. *"She's A Fool"*
C. *"It's My Party"*
D. *"Judy's Turn to Cry"*
Score: 3 points

(342) **Q: Besides the Big Bopper, Buddy Holly and Waylon Jennings, who was also invited to be on that fateful flight which crashed in a cornfield in Iowa?**
A. *Dion*
B. *Bobby Vee*
C. *Gene Pitney*
D. *Sonny Bono*
Score: 10 points

(343) **Q: According to his commanding officer, how was Elvis's performance rated as a GI during time in the army?**
A. *"Below average"*
B. *"Average"*
C. *"Above average"*
D. *"Superior"*
Score: 10 points

(344) **Q: How long did it take former royal teen Bob Guidio to come up with the words and music to "Sherry"?**
A. *He wrote it between sessions in about 2 hours.*
B. *He wrote the song for his daughter Sherry in 10 minutes.*
C. *It took about 15 minutes to write the song.*
D. *Actually, the song was "in the making" for over 7 years.*
Score: 7 points

(345) **Q: How old was Tommy Roe when he wrote "Shiela"?**
A. *21*
B. *18*
C. *16*
D. *14*
Score: 7 points

(346) **Q: Name the song that Elvis said was ". . . the stupidest thing I've ever heard . . ."**
A. *"Tiptoe Through the Tulips"*
B. *"Surfin' Bird"*
C. *"Yellow Submarine"*
D. *"Monster Mash"*
Score: 10 points

(347) **Q: What famous group in their own right played all the background instruments for the Chiffons on "He's So Fine"?**
A. *The Tokens*
B. *The Happenings*
C. *The Zombies*
D. *The Cookies*
Score: 10 points

Tom Moffatt with Bo Diddly.

(348) Q: Who was the 1st British female of the rock era to have a #1 hit in America?
A. Shelly Fabares
B. Olivia Newton John
C. Petula Clark
D. Anne Murray
Score: 5 points

(349) Q: Elvis had a hit with "Such A Night." Who had the original?
A. Elvis had the original.
B. Clyde McPhatter and the Drifters
C. The Clovers
D. The Nightriders
Score: 9 points

Questions

(350) Q: Where did Tommy James get the name "Mony, Mony" for the hit of the same name?
A. Mony is short for money.
B. "Mutual of New York" Insurance.
C. Mony is a slang term for young lady.
D. Tommy wrote the song about an old girlfriend named Marie but didn't want to be too obvious about it. (Tommy only recently revealed this fact on the Ron Foster Show.)
Score: 8 points

(351) Q: Where did Ernie K. Doe discover the sheet music for his hit "Mother-In-Law"?
A. As strange as it may seem, the song was actually written by his wife with help from her mother.
B. In a trash can.
C. Ernie wrote the song in a dream after an argument with his wife concerning her mother's dog.
D. The song was written by Ernie's father-in-law.
Score: 6 points

(352) Q: Who first recorded "Hello Mary Lou"?
A. Rick Nelson
B. Gene Pitney
C. Neil Sedaka
D. Roy Orbison
Score: 10 points

MY DAYS AS A ROCK 'N' ROLL "SUPERSTAR!"

OK, I was never a superstar. I just thought I was. There is something psychologically addictive about having girls throwing their clothes at you when you are singing and that is exactly what I was doing in 1963 just before the Beatles hit the states. We had begun as a group called The Twilights, consisting of three guys and three guitars with me as the lead singer. We played around our Texas City, Texas hometown area at car dealerships, private parties . . . fun stuff. No money . . . just fun . . . and girls! Man, it is just incredible to be there singing and having girls just sit there and watch you. I loved it. The first song I ever sang at a private party was "I Got A Woman." It was the only song we knew and we played it 33 times that night.

The Twilights eventually became the Detours with three guitars, a bass, a drummer, sax and trumpet. We made "Turn on Your Lovelight" scream with rock 'n' roll fever! "Shout" was a mainstay. We slowed things down with "16 Candles" and "Donna." These were all oldies in 1963, but they were "in" and so were we. We did a hot job on "Louie Louie." I was the lead singer and rhythm guitar player and we had Hunter Lowry on lead guitar . . . he was great! Mike Cooper was also with the group as lead and rhythm guitar. Ricky Smith was our bass player. Steve Hunter was our drummer. Joe Gillespie on trumpet and John Shockey on sax and vocals. Like most groups, the members changed from time to time, but, at our peak, we were hot!

I remember how we learned our music. There was this group playing locally in Texas City at the Teen Hops which was "the" place to be on Friday night and we used to just stand next to the stage and write down the chords and the words to their music.

Their lead singer was this guy named Johnny Lee. Yeah, the Johnny Lee of "Urban Cowboy" – "Lookin' for Love" fame. They were the hottest group around and they were the mainstay of the Teen Hops. Johnny and the Roadrunners! Hot stuff. They had a full group and I never thought we could even come close to that kind of sound. Wow! So we watched. And waited.

It was a Thursday when the phone rang. It was the manager of the Teen Hops and he wanted us to play! Wow! My first reaction was an emphatic "Yes sir!" After I hung up and called all the other guys, it became apparent that I was not a great businessman; I hadn't even asked what the job payed. Oh well. Who cares? The Texas City Teen Hop on a Friday night? There would be at least 400 people there and we would be the "act." This was big stuff. I

Questions

called all my friends and we were set.

We killed 'em! I mean the girls started screaming and tossing their clothes at us and we just kind of looked at each other and it was like a dream coming true. To stand on stage and to have people stare at you . . . and dance? There is nothing like it. It can become intoxicating. For some, too intoxicating.

It is easy to see how people can get caught up in themselves when they are being told how great they are. When you can date any girl you want . . . when you get asked for your autograph while you are walking down the halls at school by someone you've known for 10 years . . . it's all pretty mind boggling and my mind was boggled. I was a stuck-up little arrogant priss! I wouldn't even talk to my girlfriend without an appointment . . . well I may be stretching the truth just a bit . . . but I am sincere in the thought that being a rock and roll star, even on a small scale, can go right to your head. Now add one ingredient we didn't have to fight . . . money! If you start believing you are greater than great and you are getting paid more than the President and you start believing all the hype . . . well, we've seen what that can do. Actually, I was lucky that the band kept reorganizing. I got frustrated. I loved the entertainment end, but I got tired of depending on other people to "make it." So, at 14 years of age, I began to get involved in the local radio station. I remember one gig we had in Alvin, Texas, about 30 minutes from Texas City. The Detours were hot in Alvin that night and we hit the road for home about 1 A.M. I had to be on the air at 4 A.M. I fell asleep on the air at 8:10 A.M. and almost lost my radio gig. I had to make a decision – a rock and roll band or rock and roll on the radio? But, there was one more gig to do.

This guy had a record out and it was hot locally . . . "Eternally" by a guy named Johnny Winters. He was appearing at a special version of a Texas City Teen Hop, and we were booked at an Elk's Lodge in LaMarque, Texas, just a few miles away. Great! We knew the night would be a flop. This new guy was hot. He had a real 45 record out and was in our home turf. His "room" was bigger . . . we were just the local band . . . I was not looking forward to the night.

8:30 P.M. We were playing "Barbara Ann" to an audience of 12. I was losing that big ego.

9 P.M. Fourteen people had come to watch the "incredible Detours."

10 P.M. The place was packed! We had someone counting heads in Texas City and the figures were in. By 11 P.M. we had over 900 people in the audi-

ence and in Texas City they had just over 800. It was a great night for Johnny Winters . . . and a great night for us. I mean that room jammed! We did "Turn on Your Lovelight" for almost an hour non-stop. "Louie, Louie." "Shout!" The crowd went nuts. So did we.

After that gig, it was like we had done it all. Now I realize that we were a local bunch of kids who had a local following . . . but . . . hey . . . it was fun . . . we got paid good money . . . and I learned not to be a snob . . . eventually . . . not yet. When the band finally broke up, I was officially "Mr. Nobody." What goes around comes around and all those people I had snobbed, snobbed me back. I deserved it.

ONE FINAL LOOK BACK. . . .

I can't help but think that the Detours were never intended to really "make it." We had scheduled a recording session to do our remake of "Love Light," and were on our way to a Houston recording studio in two cars. I didn't know my way around in the "Big H". The guy driving the car in front of me had a flat tire . . . we passed them . . . and we were separated and lost. We never made the session. For years I wondered what would have happened if we had recorded our version of that song. I do know this. It would have cooked. We might have had ourselves a hit record. The odds are we would have. The climate was right.

Page 105

Questions

I would have remained a stuck-up snob and probably would have gotten rich and more stuck on myself and stuck on no telling what else . . . and I would have probably become one of "them." A sad headline. A grim statistic. I have that impulsive personality with which I would have most likely fried myself with rock 'n' roll and the "glory" it brings. For years I thought of what "fate" had caused me to miss. Now, looking back, I can see that it was Someone looking over me. I have found true peace . . . a peace I never knew existed. I love my Christian walk. I have happiness. And let me not forget . . . I still have rock 'n' roll! A side of it I can handle. A handle on rock 'n' roll I love. I have a wife I have loved for over 24 years. We have a beautiful 20 year old daughter who has made me so proud. And, instead of girls throwing their clothes at me . . . I've got a little 11 year old guy named Chance who throws a mean baseball. Who could ask for more?

THE DETOURS

Here's a look at one version of The Detours. Left to right: David McQuarrie, Hunter Lowry, Rickey Hamilton (me), Ricky Smith, and Steve Hunter. This shot was printed in the local paper and taken just before our first Teen Hop appearance. Why did I have to be the one to make the funky curl? Good grief.

David and I played rhythm guitar and sang. Hunter Lowry had to be one of the coolest guitarists I've ever heard. He just "had it." Ricky Smith was the best bass player I've ever worked with. The girls thought he looked like Paul McCartney. In fact, one of our mainstay songs was Ricky playing "Exodus" on bass! For many years he and I were best friends. Steve Hunter was just great on the drums and the last time I saw him at our 20 year reunion, he was still drumming in Los Angeles. Wherever you are guys . . . those were some fun days, eh? Playing in the rock band brings back some of the most memorable and happiest days of my life.

Questions

BEATLE SOUNDS-A lively show and Beatle-style music by the "Detours" will be onstage for the Noon Optimist "Teen Hop" May 1 at Nessler Recreation Center. Billed as Texas City's answer to the famous "Beatles," the "Detours" are shown above, left to right, David McQuarrie, Hunter Lowry, Ricky Hamilton, Ricky Smith, and Steve Hunter.

(353) Q: <u>Time</u> Magazine said: there is no singer in modern history who has not been influenced by him." He was Eddie Cochran's favorite singer. Who is he?

A. *Elvis Presley*
B. *Ray Charles*
C. *Johnny Mathis*
D. *Little Richard*
Score: 8 points

(354) Q: True or False? Between 1957 and 1964 Little Richard left the music field, studied religion and became a minister?
Score: 6 points

(355) Q: What #1 Elvis song was first recorded by Jerry Lewis (The Comedian)?

A. *"Are You Lonesome Tonight"? – as a novelty*
B. *"It's Now or Never"*
C. *"Jailhouse Rock" – in a movie short*
D. *This is a trick question.*
Score: 7 points

"I think that bathing suit looks good on you bob!" "Thanks Jim."

(356) Q: What Elvis #1 hit was first recorded by Al Jolson?

A. *"Are You Lonesome Tonight"?*
B. *"It's Now or Never"*
C. *"Jailhouse Rock"*
D. *This is another stupid trick question.*
Score: 8 points

(357) Q: When Dick Clark's "Caravan of Stars" reached Cincinnati, Paul, of Paul and Paula walked out. Who sang alone with Paula for the next two weeks of the tour?

A. *Dick Clark*
B. *Bobby Vee was brought in.*
C. *Chris Montez*
D. *Freddie Cannon*
Score: 10 points

Questions

(358) Q: What was Rock 'n' Roll's first tragedy song?
  A. *"The Three Bells"*
  B. *"Tragedy"*
  C. *"Teen Angel"*
  D. *"Dead Man's Curve"*
  Score: 8 points

(359) Q: What was the first #1 single of the sixties?
  A. *"Big Bad John"*
  B. *"El Paso"*
  C. *"The Race Is On"*
  D. *"Bring It on Home to Me"*
  Score: 10 points

Questions

(360) Q: What was the first record to enter the British charts at #1?
  A. *"She Loves You"*
  B. *"Sittin' on the Dock of the Bay"*
  C. *"Jailhouse Rock"*
  D. *"All Shook Up"*
  Score: 10 points

(361) Q: Who co-wrote "Sweet Soul Music" with its singer Arthur Conley?
  A. *Otis Redding*
  B. *Sam Cooke*
  C. *Marvin Gaye*
  D. *Smokey Robinson*
  Score: 10 points

Do not try this at home.

(362) Q: Who wrote Bobby Goldsboro's classic #1 hit "Honey"?
A. *Bobby Goldboro*
B. *Bobby Russell*
C. *Sonny Trockmorton*
D. *Don Cook*
Score: 10 points

(363) Q: The group was called Booker T. and the M.G.'s. What does the M.G. stand for?

Tom Moffatt with Dodie Stevens, Bobby Rydell and Chubby Checker.

A. *Making (it) Good*
B. *Memphis Gold*
C. *Memphis Group*
D. *Motown Gold*
Score: 7 points

(364) Q: What was Motown's first girl group?
A. *The Ronnettes*
B. *The Marvelettes*
C. *The Shirelles*
D. *The Chiffons*
Score: 10 points

(365) Q: Which song of the rock era was inspired by Phil Spector's dad's epitaph?
A. *"Goodnight My Love"*
B. *"See You Later Alligator"*
C. *"A Thousand Stars"*
D. *"To Know Him Is To Love Him"*
Score: 6 points

(366) Q: Which one of the Monkeys never played a note before joining the group?
A. *Not one played an instrument.*
B. *Mickey Dolenz*
C. *Davy Jones*
D. *They all played instruments.*
Score: 7 points

(367) Q: Who finally mixed the mountains of tape which eventually became the Beatles' "Let It Be" LP?

A. Paul McCartney
B. John Lennon
C. Dick Clark
D. Phil Spector
Score: 4 points

(368) Q: What were some of the so-called signs that Paul McCartney was dead?
Score: 4 points for each correct answer
Answers: (next page)

(369) Q: What popular female singer of the sixties added backing vocals to Mary Wells' and Marvin Gaye's early recordings?

A. Dee Dee Sharp
B. Martha Reeves
C. Diana Ross
D. Gladys Knight
Score: 10 points

Do not open your eyes!

(370) Q: What was Bob Dylan's claim to musical fame before he became a star in his own right?

A. *There was none.*
B. *He played harmonica for Harry Belafonti recording sessions.*
C. *He played harmonica on several Beach Boys' recordings.*
D. *He played the harmonica on "Baby Don't Go".*
Score: 10 points

(371) Q: Why didn't Elvis appear on "American Bandstand"?

A. *Elvis was already an established artist and did not need the exposure.*
B. *Dick Clark and Elvis did not get along.*
C. *The Colonel's asking price for an Elvis appearance was too high.*
D. *Elvis was never invited to appear because the Colonel would not return Dick's phone calls.*
Score: 6 points

(372) Q: How much did "American Bandstand" pay the name performers to appear on the show?

A. *$1,000*
B. *$1,388*
C. *$138*
D. *$56*

Score: 10 points

(373) Q: Who wrote "Rockin' Pneumonia and the Boogie Woogie Flu"?

A. *Johnny Rivers*
B. *Huey "Piano" Smith*
C. *Little Richard*
D. *Fats Domino*

Score: 8 points

(374) Q: Who said: "The first time I ever sang a song on a stage I did `Long Tall Sally.' Ever since I heard Little Richard's version, I've been imitating him"?

A. *Pat Boone*
B. *Paul McCartney*
C. *Michael Jackson*
D. *John Lennon*

Score: 8 points

Questions

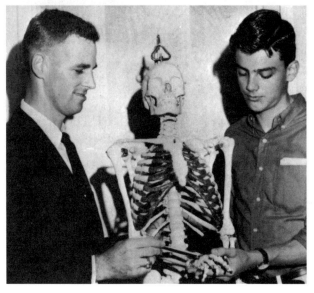

I Wanna Hold Your Hand.

Answers to Paul McCartney question: (1) Paul was the only one barefoot and out of step on the cover of "Abbey Road". (2) A hand is held over Paul's head on the "Sgt. Pepper" – a sign of death in some cultures. (3) "Revolution #9" played backwards sounds like a car crash. (4) The introduction of Billy Shears who was supposedly going to take Paul's place. (5) Paul is supposedly buried under his guitar on the "Sgt. Pepper" cover. (6) "Come Together" contains the words "come together over me," a sign of a funeral. (7) The line "one and one and one is three" from "Come Together". There may have been others but the bottom line is, Paul is alive and well.

(375) **Q: What song saved "American Bandstand" according to Dick Clark?**
A. *"The Twist"*
B. *"Quarter to Three"*
C. *"Palisades Park"*
D. *"The Stroll"*
Score: 10 points

(376) **Q: What was Frankie Avalon forced to do during the recording of his Top Ten hit "Dede Dinah"?**
A. *Frankie was forced to eat three hamburgers before recording to get a full sound.*
B. *He recorded the song while standing on his head for special effects.*
C. *Frankie was forced to sing the song with a large rat running loose in the studio. According to some sources the rat was placed there by Annette Funicello as a payback prank.*
D. *He was forced to hold his nose while singing the song.*
Score: 8 points

Questions

(377) **Q: Who influenced Simon and Garfunkle more than any other performers?**
A. *Laurel and Hardy*
B. *The Righteous Brothers*
C. *The Everly Brothers*
D. *The Belmonts*
Score: 3 points

A swingin' couple.

(378) **Q: Name the first black group to reach #1 on the pop charts.**
A. *The Coasters with "Charlie Brown"*
B. *The Platters with "The Great Pretender"*
C. *The Platters with "Smoke Gets in Your Eyes"*
D. *The Coasters with "Yakety Yak"*
Score: 9 points

(379) Q: What group has been called "The East Coast's version of the Beach Boys"?
A. *Joe Dee and the Starlighters*
B. *The Lettermen*
C. *The Four Seasons*
D. *The Crew Cuts*
Score: 6 points

(380) Q: They were originally named "The Four Arms" in 1954. Their first hit was in 1964. They are still together. Name that group.
A. *The Four Seasons*
B. *The Four Tops*
C. *The Four Preps*
D. *The Outsiders*
Score: 10 points

(381) Q: What was Dick Clark's estimated financial net worth in October, 1990?
A. *$100 million*
B. *$150 million*
C. *$1 billion*
D. *$210 million*
Score: 9 points

(382) Q: On what program did Elvis make his national TV debut?
A. *The Ed Sullivan Show*
B. *The Dorsey Brother's Stage Show*
C. *The Grand Ole Opry*
D. *The Steve Allen Show*
Score: 9 points

(383) Q: What was Aretha's only #1 song listed below?
A. *This is another trick question. Aretha had more than one number one song.*
B. *"Respect"*
C. *"A Natural Woman"*
D. *"Since You've Been Gone"*
Score: 6 points

Touchdown!

The Joneses in the fall of 1966. The Joneses were a local legend in the New England area between '66 and '74. From Left to Right: Roby Zicarro, Jo D'Angelo, Lower Right, Jimmy D'Angelo, Upper Right: Marty Norris. The band later changed it's name to Mad Angel from 1974-78.

(384)   Q: Name at least five Beatle songs on which Ringo sang lead?
Answers: Next page

(385)   Q: What famous singer co-wrote the Searcher's "Needles and Pins"?
   A. *Glen Campbell*
   B. *Neil Sedaka*
   C. *Sonny Bono*
   D. *Gene Pitney*
   Score: 10 points

Answers from previous page: "Matchbox," "Honey Don't," "Act Naturally," "What Goes On," "Yellow Submarine," "With a Little Help from My Friends," "Octopus's Garden". 5 points for every one you guessed!!!

(386)   Q: **Which notorious rebel was claimed by critics in the mid fifties to be " . . . leading a rebellion intent on destroying the fabric of society"?**
   A. *Elvis*
   B. *Little Richard*
   C. *Jerry Lee Lewis*
   D. *Bill Haley*
   Score: 10 points

1967-Marty of The Jonses a club in Western Massachusetts

(387) **Q: What was Johnny Rivers's only #1 song?**
A. *"Memphis"*
B. *"Poor Side of Town"*
C. *"Seventh Son"*
D. *"Baby I Need Your Lovin'"*
Score: 5 points

(389) **Q: What was Robert Parker's claim to fame?**
A. *He was the drummer on the hit "Let There Be Drums".*
B. *He was Elvis Presley's barber when he was in the Army.*
C. *He sang the hit "Barefootin'".*
D. *He wrote "Eve of Destruction".*
Score: 7 points

(390) **Q: What song officially put Gene Pitney on the Rock 'n' Roll map?**
A. *"Only Love Can Break a Heart"*
B. *"Town Without Pity"*
C. *"It Hurts To Be In Love"*
D. *"Half-Heaven, Half Heartache"*
Score: 6 points

(391) **Q: In the Beach Boys' hit "Barbara Ann," where did they meet her?**
A. *At her home*
B. *At her front door*
C. *At a twist party*
D. *At a dance*
Score: 5 points

Tom Moffatt and Brenda Lee

(392) **Q: Kenny Rogers's group was . . .**
A. *The Fifth Dimension*
B. *The Fifth Edition*
C. *The First Edition*
D. *The Last Edition*
Score: 5 points

(393) **Q: What was the Marvelettes' highest charted song?**
A. *"Shop Around"*
B. *"Dedicated to the One I Love"*
C. *"Soldier Boy"*
D. *"Please Mr. Postman"*
Score: 10 points

(394) Q: What is Booker T's last name?
A. Tendale
B. Thomas
C. Smith
D. Jones
Score: 3 points

(395) Q: What kind of people inhabited "Lucy in the Sky With Diamonds"?
A. Mellow Yellow people
B. Strawberry people
C. Rocking chair people
D. Rocking horse people
Score: 5 points

(396) Q: What was the Whos' highest charted song?
A. "Won't Get Fooled Again"
B. "Magic Bus"
C. "I Can See For Miles"
D. "Free Ride"
Score: 10 points

(397) Q: Who produced Mary Hopkin's hit "Those Were The Days"?
A. Phil Spector
B. John Lennon
C. Paul McCartney
D. George Harrison
Score: 7 points

(398) Q: Eddie Floyd had a hit with "Knock On Wood." Who had the original?
A. The Clovers
B. The Nightriders
C. The Bellnotes
D. This is another trick question. Eddie Floyd had the original.
Score: 6 points

Fake dogs.

(399) **Q: From whom did the Beatles get the idea for their name?**
A. It came from the idea of a rock 'n' roll beat.
B. They got the idea from watching an old Japanese "B" movie entitled "The Invasion of the Monster Beetles".
C. They took the idea from Buddy Holly and the Crickets.
D. Paul got the idea for the name while putting together a bug collection in high school. He collected an amazing 400 Beatles from all parts of the world. After winning his #1 prize ribbon, he was quoted as saying: "If I ever get into rock and roll, I too will be a beetle."
Score: 7 points

(400) **Q: James Taylor had a hit with "Handy Man." Who had the original?**
A. Clyde McPhatter
B. Jewel Akins
C. Jimmy Jones
D. Kenny Rogers
Score: 6 points

Questions

(401) **Q: What was Johnny Rivers' first hit?**
A. "Maybelline"
B. "Memphis"
C. "Poor Side of Town"
D. "Seventh Son"
Score: 7 points

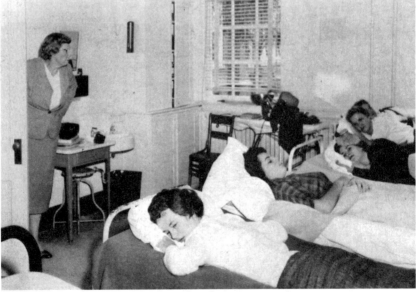

Who made that disgusting noise?

(402) **Q: What was the Drifter's highest charted song?**

A. *"Since I Fell for You"*
B. *"Under the Boardwalk"*
C. *"Soul Man"*
D. *"Save the Last Dance for Me"*
Score: 10 points

Shindigger Dancers

(403) **Q: How did "Teen Angel" die?**

A. *She was run over by a car.*
B. *She was run over by a train.*
C. *She was run over by a truck.*
D. *She died in a motorcycle wreck.*
Score: 6 points

(404) **Q: What was the highest charted song of Dusty Springfield?**

A. *"Downtown"*
B. *"You Don't Have to Say You Love Me"*
C. *"I Say a Little Prayer for You"*
D. *"Will You Still Love Me Tomorrow"?*
Score: 7 points

(405) **Q: What was the first hit for the Dixie Cups?**

A. *"Chapel of Love"*
B. *"My Boy Lollipop"*
C. *"Don't Say Nothin' Bad About My Baby"*
D. *"Will You Still Love Me Tomorrow"?*
Score: 7 points

(406) **Q: What was Gene Chandler's highest rated song?**

A. *"Groovy Situation"*
B. *"Tossin' and Turnin'"*
C. *"Summertime"*
D. *"Duke of Earl"*
Score: 5 points

Questions

(407) Q: What was the first hit for the Chiffons?
A. "Soldier Boy"
B. "Will You Still Love Me Tomorrow"?
C. "One Fine Day"
D. "He's So Fine"
Score: 10 points (Hey, I'm giving folks a chance to catch up)

(408) Q: Where was Englebert Humperdinck born?
A. England
B. Australia
C. Holland
D. India
Score: 7 points

(409) Q: In the early sixties, who did a French newspaper mistakenly refer to as a "32 year old midget"?
A. Brenda Lee
B. Marcie Blaine
C. Johnny Rivers
D. Hank Ballard
Score: 9 points

Chubby Checker "Mr. Twist" and Tom Moffatt

(410) Q: In what year did the new Christy Minstrels record their top 20 version of Paul Anka's classic "You're Havin' My Baby"?
A. 1972
B. 1973
C. 1974
D. This is a ridiculous trick question
Score: 10 points

(411) Q: What did Martha Reeves of the Vandellas consider the highlight of her career by 1990 according to an interview on the Ron Foster program?
A. The fact that "Dancin' in the Street" had been used as a TV commercial
B. The fact that "her career was coming back to life . . ."
C. The fact that one of her songs was used to chase Manuel Noriega out of hiding ("Nowhere to Run")
D. The birth of her first grandchild who was named Vanessa after the "Vandellas"
Score: 10 points

(412)   Q: In what 1967 movie did Ringo Starr make his
        solo acting debut?
        A. *"Candy"*
        B. *"The Candyman"*
        C. *"I Want Candy"*
        D. *"A Look at the Beatles from Where I Sat"* – *a documentary*
           (shown in Britain only)
        Score: 10 points

(413)   Q: Who permanently replaced Brian Wilson as a
        Beach Boy in 1965?
        A. *Glen Campbell*
        B. *Bruce Johnston*
        C. *Mike Love*
        D. *Hank Aaron*
        Score: 10 points

(414)   Q: Elvis was one of twin boys born on January 8, 1935. What was
        his twin brother's name?
        A. *Jesse Aaron*
        B. *Jesse Garon*
        C. *Jesse Lewis*
        D. *Jesse Melvin*
        Score: 10 points

Questions

Robin Luke, Connie Francis, and Tom Moffatt.

(415) Q: Where did Otis Redding go after he left the dock of the bay?
A. He went home.
B. He rode away on a boat.
C. He went to San Francisco.
D. He stayed on the dock.
Score: 10 points

(416) Q: Who was Arty Garr?
A. Arthur Conley
B. Art Garfunkle
C. Hank Ballard
D. Rod Stewart
Score: 9 points

(417) Q: Who had the original version of "Hang on Sloopy?"
A. The McCoys
B. The Victors
C. The Vibrations
D. The Pendletones
Score: 10 points

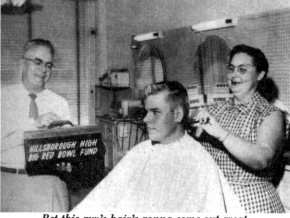

Bet this guy's hair's gonna come out great.

(418) Q: Who sang "The Twist", "Finger Poppin' Time", and "Let's Go, Let's Go"?
A. Hank Ballard
B. Chubby Checker
C. Van Morrison and Them
D. Danny and the Juniors
Score: 9 points

(419) Q: What group was known at one time as the Pendletones?
A. The Beach Boys
B. The Rolling Stones
C. The Beatles
D. The Who
Score: 10 points

(420) Q: What is Tiny Tim's daughter's name?
A. Delta
B. Rose
C. Tulip
D. Petunia
Score: 9 points

(421) Q: The Rascals were said to have "Blue Eyed Soul." How many members of the group actually had blue eyes?

A. *Every member – this is how the term came about.*
B. *None*
C. *Half the group*
D. *No one ever noticed, making this just another trick question.*
Score: 7 points

(422) Q: What are Seals and Crofts' first names?

A. *Phil and Don*
B. *Santo and Johnny*
C. *Jim and Dash*
D. *Sammy and Wilburn*
Score: 7 points

(423) Q: What city is the Steve Miller band from?

A. *Detroit*
B. *Chicago*
C. *Dallas*
D. *San Francisco*
Score: 9 points

Wanna pop?

Bonus Time!

Name each of these famous actors for 10 points each.

Questions

Answers: Top Left: Katherine Hepburn, Top Center: Clark Gable, Top Right: Sammy Davis, Jr., Center Left: John Wayne, Bottom Left: Leonard Nimoy (Spock), Bottom Right: Marilyn Monroe.

(424) Q: What was Bobby Darin's highest charted song?
A. "Splish Splash"
B. "Dream Lover"
C. "Mac the Knife"
D. "Queen of the Hop"
Score: 10 points

(425) Q: What was the 10th commandment in the original version of the Moonglow's classic "10 Commandments of Love"?
A. Thou shalt only love me.
B. Thou shalt remember thy vows.
C. Thou shalt be mine.
D. There was no 10th commandment in the original.
Score: 9 points

(426) Q: What is the sequel to the fifties song "A Thousand Miles Away"?
A. "El Paso"
B. "500 Miles Away from Home"
C. "Daddy's Home"
D. "Angel Baby"
Score: 10 points

(427) Q: What kind of house did Johnny B. Goode live in?
A. Clay and mud
B. Brick and wood
C. Earth and mud
D. Earth and wood
Score: 8 points

(428) Q: What was the dance done to Dale Hawkin's "Suzy Q"?
A. The Stroll
B. The Jitterbug
C. The Circle Dance
D. The Bunny Hop
Score: 10 points

Pat Sajak of "Wheel of Fortune" and Ron Foster. (Pat is like I am about tying ties).

(429) **Q: Name the most popular American group of the late sixties who had their own version of Dale Hawkin's "Suzy Q."**
A. *There was never a remake*
B. *The Beach Boys*
C. *Creedence Clearwater Revival*
D. *The Turtles*
Score: 5 points

(430) **Q: Where did the Monotones get the idea for the melody to their hit "Book of Love"?**
A. *From a Coca Cola commercial*
B. *From a Bayer Aspirin commercial*
C. *It was an original song*
D. *From a Pepsodent commercial*
Score: 10 points

(431) **Q: Two Little Eva versions of "The Locomotion" were eventually released, one with hand claps and one without. On the clapping version, who clapped?**
A. *Little Eva*
B. *Carole King*
C. *Dick Clark*
D. *The Cookies*
Score: 10 points

Ho, Ho, Ho.

(432) **Q: How did the Poni-Tails get their name?**
A. *They all had poni-tails.*
B. *Poni-tails were in fashion when the song was recorded.*
C. *They attended the same equestrian academy class where they came up with the name.*
D. *It was the name of Gene Autry's horse, and he was their idol.*
Score: 8 points

(433) Q: How old was Frankie Avalon when he signed his first recording contract?
A. 6
B. 7
C. 11
D. 14
Score: 10 points

(434) Q: What is the best selling song of the rock era? (This does not include Christmas songs).
A. *"Hound Dog"*
B. *"Rock Around the Clock"*
C. *"The Twist"*
D. *"It's Now or Never"*
Score: 10 points

(435) Q: Who wrote the classic "Love Is Strange" under his wife's name?
A. *Sonny Bono*
B. *Bo Diddley*
C. *Dick Clark*
D. *Gene Pitney*
Score: 10 points

Dan Stevens and Ron Foster. Dan is one of America's most gifted morning show hosts.

(436) Q: What is significant about the number 53310761?
A. *It was Paul Anka's private telephone number in 1963.*
B. *It was Elvis's serial number in the U.S. Army.*
C. *The number has no special significance.*
D. *When added together, the numbers, easily seen on the cover of "Sgt. Pepper" would have indicated Paul's last birthday . . . thus the "Paul is dead" rumors.*
Score: 7 points

(437) Q: What instrument did Bill Black play?
A. *Drums*
B. *Keyboard*
C. *Bass*
D. *Drums, keyboard, bass, and violin*
Score: 6 points

(438) Q: What Paul Anka song is considered by many critics to be the most humanistic, "self-centered" song ever recorded?
A. *"You're Havin' My Baby"*
B. *"Diana"*
C. *"My Way"*
D. *"Put Your Head on My Shoulder"*
Score: 6 points

(439) Q: In the spring of 1959, Henry Mancini had what #1 album in the country?
A. *"Theme from Rawhide"*
B. *"Theme from Batman"*
C. *"Theme from Peter Gunn"*
D. *"Theme from Superman"*
Score: 10 points

"Look! An oncoming train. Will you really go back to get my Senior ring?"

Questions

(440) Q: What label did Rufus Thomas record on before he recorded the "Funky Chicken"?
A. *Mowtown*
B. *Delta*
C. *Double Barrel*
D. *Sun*
Score: 10 points

(441) Q: What time was Susie supposed to be home in "Wake Up Little Susie"?
A. *10pm*
B. *9pm*
C. *11pm*
D. *Midnight at the latest*
Score: 7 points

(442) Q: What TV show drew an incredible 54 million viewers in 1956?
A. *"Eisenhower Lands" (narrative by Walter Cronkite and featuring a short interview with Elvis who was in the U.S. Army)*
B. *Elvis' appearance on Ed Sullivan*
C. *Live coverage of the Dempsey/Sullivan fight in which former boxer Jackie Wilson provided ringside commentary*
D. *"Rock, Rock, Rock" shown for the very first time on TV*
Score: 5 points

(443) **Q: Who was the shortest Beatle?**
A. *John*
B. *Paul*
C. *George*
D. *Ringo*
Score: 4 points

(444) **Q: How big was the diamond on Little Egypt's toe?**
A. *As big as can be*
B. *As big as her heart*
C. *As big as Texas*
D. *As big as my love for you*
Score: 5 points

(445) **Q: Where did Bobby Darin get the idea for "Splish Splash"?**
A. *While flying in the house, his mother landed in the tub.*
B. *The idea came from Dick Clark's mother.*
C. *Bobby came up with the idea.*
D. *From Murry the K's mother*
Score: 10 points

Sound Generation Singers prepared for their first record release.

The Shirelles owe me one . . .

It was 1972 and I was an afternoon drive personality for a Top 40 cooker in Houston, Texas and also the Program Director. Across the hall from our station was this UHF television station and, at about 12:30 in the afternoon as I was preparing to go on the air, one of the producers of a live TV program came running into my office.

"Ron! You gotta help me!"

"What's happening"?

"We have the Shirelles about to go on live and they didn't bring a tape or record or anything. We are going to interview them, then, we want them to sing one of their hits. Do you have one I can borrow?

"Man! We stopped playing the Shirelles when the disco thing hit. I don't think we even have one in the building . . . let me check." I was a little put out. The Shirelles? They had gone out with the hula hoop.

"Hey man . . . hurry . . . we got about three minutes and I gotta have a song!"

I ran to the music library and looked under the "S's".

"Here, play a Supremes' song. No one will know the difference." I was kind of a smart mouth.

"Come on man!"

"OK. Just a second. Let me see. Here you go. Shirelles. 'Will You Still Love Me Tomorrow.' That was one of their big hits."

"Oh man. Thanks! You saved my life."

And he was off in a flash to the TV station. Thinking back, I didn't even have enough interest to walk across the hall and get a glimpse. The Shirelles? History. Disco was in. That old rock was out. Shows you how smart I was.

It was about an hour later when a rather dejected producer came back into the radio station just before I went on the air.

"Thanks a lot, Ron." He said it rather sarcastically as he handed me the old 45.

"What's the matter? Was it scratchy or something"? I asked, now really interested.

"You got a minute"?

We walked across the hall and strolled into the booth where the live show had been taped for future reference. It had gone on the air live.

"Well, thank you girls . . . and now let's go back a few years and hear one of your big hits "Will You Still Love Me Tomorrow?"

The camera zoomed in close up as the girls began to move with the music and then sing the words. It was about half way into the song when it happened!

"Tonight you're mine completely . . . completely . . . completely . . . com . . . comp . . . comp . . . comp . . . comp . . . comp . ."

The record had hit a crack and there were the Shirelles trying to lip sync to a song that was skipping. Finally, mercifully, the camera faded to black.

"Hey guys. I didn't know the song would skip. Honest. It wasn't my fault . . . I . . ."

The producer threw the record at me as I ducked. I pretended to run from the studio, picked up the record, and, as he turned his head back toward the TV monitors, threw the record at him and hit him in the back of the head. We both got a good laugh out of it.

TO THE SHIRELLES:

Sorry girls. I love you. I'm glad you're back. Honest. I didn't know it would skip.

(446)   Q: What did Charlie Brown call his teacher?
A. *Geek*
B. *Nurd*
C. *Goofy hat*
D. *Daddy-o*
Score: 4 points

(447)   Q: In Jack Scott's classic "My True Love," how does he get his true love?
A. *He talks to her on the phone.*
B. *He sees her at school.*
C. *He prays for her.*
D. *He climbs a tree with her.*
Score: 9 points

(448)   Q: As a kid, Eddie Hodges was on the "$64,000 Question" with whom?
A. *June Lockhart*
B. *Wayne Newton*
C. *Mickey Mantle*
D. *John Glen*
Score: 10 points

What a cool car.

"I'll buy it if that 'Babe Machine' clause stays in the contract ... heh, heh."

(449) Q: In the late Bobby Bloom's "Montego Bay" when will Vernon meet him?
   A. In the midnight hour
   B. When the Borax lands
   C. When the Bo-ac lands
   D. When the Borris lands
   Score: 6 points

(450) Q: If all the leaves are brown, what color is the sky in "California Dreamin'"?
   A. Gray
   B. Blue
   C. Red
   D. Yellow
   Score: 7 points

(451) Q: What was the highest charted song of Mary Wells?
   A. "Please Mr. Postman"
   B. "My Guy"
   C. "You'll Lose a Good Thing"
   D. "Dancin' in the Street"
   Score: 9 points

Captain Trivia in my '58 cool jacket.

(452)   Q: What was the highest charted song of Paul Revere and the Raiders?
A. *"Just Like Me"*
B. *"Kicks"*
C. *"Indian Reservation"*
D. *"Good Thing"*
Score: 10 points

(453)   Q: What was the first hit for Gladys Knight and the Pips?
A. *"Midnight Train to Houston"*
B. *"Midnight Train to Georgia"*
C. *"I Heard it Through the Grapevine"*
D. *"Every Beat Of My Heart"*
Score: 10 points

(454)   Q: Who was the Beatles' first producer?
A. *Phil Spector*
B. *Brian Esptein*
C. *George Martin*
D. *Paul Harrison*
Score: 7 points

(455)   Q: What state was Janice Joplin from?
A. *Pennsylvania*
B. *Arizona*
C. *Texas*
D. *California*
Score: 6 points

(456)   Q: Where was Mick Jagger from?
A. *Sidney, Australia*
B. *London, England*
C. *New York, New York*
D. *Kent, England*
Score: 9 points

(457)   Q: Who was Kathy Young's backup group on the hit "A Thousand Stars"?
A. *The Ad Libs*
B. *The Innocents*
C. *Kathy Young played all the instruments on the song.*
D. *The Crescents*
Score: 9 points

(458) Q: Who originally recorded "That's All Right Mama"?
A. Arthur "Big Boy" Crudup
B. Edward "Bad Boy" Harrison
C. Jeremy "Boo Boo" Barklay
D. JoJo "Mad Dog" Henry
Score: 10 points

(459) Q: Who is Gene Chandler's girlfriend in the "Duke of Earl"?
A. The Duchess of the kingdom
B. The Duchess of the Parliament
C. The Duchess of Earl
D. The Duchess of Pearl
Score: 5 points

(460) Q: What was Tommy Roe's first hit?
A. "Shiela"
B. "Peggy Sue"
C. "Everybody"
D. "Dizzy"
Score: 8 points

(461) Q: Who is Carole Klein?
A. Shelly Fabares
B. Carol Lawrence
C. Carole King
D. Cathy Young
Score: 9 points

(462) Q: What was Bob Dylan's highest charted song that he sang himself?
A. "Blowin' in the Wind"
B. "Like A Rolling Stone"
C. "Lay Lady Lay"
D. "Knockin' on Heaven's Door"
Score: 5 points

Oops!

Questions

(463) Q: **Who was the lead singer for the Dave Clark Five?**
A. *Mike Smith*
B. *Paul Jones*
C. *Paul Smith*
D. *Mike Jones*
Score: 10 points

(464) Q: **What brought Elvis the charge that he: " . . . is lawless and leading our youth to juvenile delinquency"?**
A. *His sideburns*
B. *The fact that the letters of his name, when mixed up spell "Evils"*
C. *His movie "Jailhouse Rock"*
D. *The song "Love Me Tender"*
Score: 10 points

(465) Q: **Who gave this philosophy to Mick Jagger: "You should never sing the words out very clearly . . . keep 'em guessing at what you are singing about"?**
A. *Keith Moon*
B. *John Lennon*
C. *Little Richard*
D. *Fats Domino*
Score: 10 points

(466) Q: **Name at least four names used in the "Name Game."**
Score: 5 points each!!!

(467) Q: **Columbia Records had been the showcase for Andy Williams and Steve Lawrence – middle of the road artists – and the label was reluctant to sign a rock 'n' roll act. In what year did Columbia "take one of the biggest risks ever," and commit itself to rock 'n' roll?**
A. *1959*
B. *1961*
C. *1963*
D. *1965*
Score: 10 points

Babby Darin with Tom Moffit. Babby's many hits included "Mac the Knife" and "Splish Splash."

(468) **Q: What rock group did Columbia sign that year?**
A. *The Animals*
B. *The Byrds*
C. *The Raiders*
D. *The Bee Gees*
Score: 10 points

(469) **Q: What is Motown's second-longest running song at #1?**
A. *"My Guy"*
B. *"I Heard It Through the Grapevine"*
C. *"Walkin' the Dog"*
D. *"Dancin' in the Street"*
Score: 10 points

Eric Burdon (Left) lead singer of the Animals along with our own Pat Clarke.

(470) **Q: When was the word "teenager" coined?**
A. *In 1956 with the "official" beginning of rock 'n' roll*
B. *Before rock and roll in the early fifties*
C. *In 1958-rock and roll's biggest year*
D. *On American Bandstand in 1959*
Score: 10 points

(471) **Q: Who called rock 'n' roll "phony and false" yet helped a close relative achieve success as a rock and roll singer?**
A. *Jerry Lewis*
B. *Frank Sinatra*
C. *Dean Martin*
D. *Ricky Ricardo*
Score: 10 points

(472) **Q: In what year did Elvis purchase Graceland?**
A. *1956*
B. *1957*
C. *1958*
D. *1959*
Score: 8 points

(473) Q: What is the highest score a song could get on "American Bandstand"?
A. 100
B. 98
C. 20
D. 10
Score: 9 points

(474) Q: What was Dion's biggest hit?
A. "Ruby Baby"
B. "The Wanderer"
C. "Runaround Sue"
D. "Abraham, Martin, and John"
Score: 10 points

(475) Q: Who sang "Little Sister"?
A. Elvis
B. Dion
C. Percy Sledge
D. Marvin Gaye
Score: 5 points

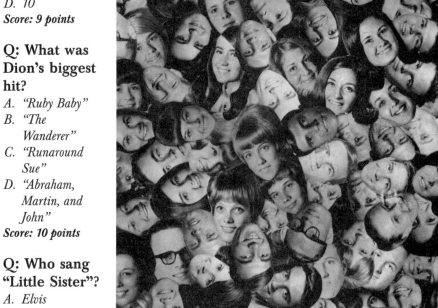
One way to get a head.

(476) Q: True or false? Elvis had a facelift?
Score: 10 points

(477) Q: Who was the first Beatle to have a #1 hit after the group broke up and what was the name of the song?
A. John with "Imagine"
B. Paul with "Uncle Albert"
C. George with "My Sweet Lord"
D. Ringo with "You're 16"
Score: 10 points

(478) Q: Producer Snuff Garrett has produced hits for Bobby Vee, Cher, Gary Lewis and more. According to him, what are his two favorite songs that he has produced?
A. *"Gypsys, Tramps, and Thieves" and "Old Rivers"*
B. *"Take Good Care of My Baby" and "This Diamond Ring"*
C. *"Rubber Ball" and "Halfbreed"*
D. *"She's Just My Style" and "This Diamond Ring"*
Score: 10 points

(479) Q: Paul Anka is from where?
A. *Brooklyn*
B. *Philadelphia*
C. *Canada*
D. *Australia*
Score: 7 points

(480) Q: According to an interview with Ron Foster, why did Roger McGuinn, lead singer of the Byrds stop wearing those square sunglasses?
A. *He got contact lenses.*
B. *They blew off while he was riding a motorcycle.*
C. *He wanted to change his image.*
D. *He gave them to Elvis as a gift.*
Score: 10 points

The Lettermen at the University of Houston. Great kissy-face music.

So _this_ is "Cruisin' U.S.A.?"

(481) Q: Who was the second Beatle to have a #1 hit after the group broke up and what was the name of the song?
A. John with "Imagine"
B. Ringo with "It Don't Come Easy"
C. George with "Give Peace a Chance"
D. Paul with "Silly Love Songs"
Score: 10 points

(482) Q: "Summertime Blues" was made famous by whom?
A. Eddie Cochran
B. Elvis
C. Bill Haley
D. Buddy Knox
Score: 7 points

(483) Q: Name at least two names the Beatles went by before they became the Beatles?
Score: 5 points for each name listed on next page

(484) Q: Name at least three acts of the rock era who had one #1 single and were never heard from again.
Score: There were many, but take 5 points for each listed on next page

(485) Q: What was Paul Anka's first recording?
A. "Diana"
B. "Put Your Head on My Shoulder"
C. "A Love Letter to Annette"
D. "Blauwildesbestfontein"
Score: 10 points

(486) Q: How many takes did it take Paul Anka to get "Diana" perfected?
A. 1
B. 2
C. 3
D. 22
Score: 10 points

(487) Q: What was Paul Anka's first #1 song?
     A. *"Diana"*
     B. *"Lonely Boy"*
     C. *"Puppy Love"*
     D. *"My Way"*
     Score: 4 points

(488) Q: True or false? The Ventures recorded their original version of "Walk Don't Run" on a home recorder?
     Score: 5 points

(483) Answers: at one time or another the Beatles went by the Quarrymen, Johnny and the Moondogs, The Silver Beatles, and The Four Everlys.

(484) Answers: the Elegants, the Singing Nun, the Hollywood Argyles, Zager and Evans, the Silhouettes, the Murmaids, Norman Greenbaum, Mungo Jerry to mention a few.

(489) Q: True or false? "There's A Moon Out Tonight" was originally released in the fifties, flopped, and was reissued in the early sixties and became a hit?
     Score: 5 points

(490) Q: In what year did Stevie Wonder drop the "Little" from his name?
     A. *1961*
     B. *1962*
     C. *1964*
     D. *1965*
     Score: 5 points

Questions

(491) Q: Eddie Kendricks and Paul Williams were two original members of the Temptations. How did they meet?
     A. *The two met on an elevator as they were running from street gangs in the Bronx. As the elevator door opened they were met by a gang and the two of them took on six gang members and won. As they celebrated, they were tempted to go back and kick the guys around a bit more . . . thus the name "Temptations."*
     B. *They were on the same high school football team.*
     C. *They were both members of the same church choir.*
     D. *They grew up in Birmingham, Alabama where Paul threw a bucket of water on Eddie, they got into a fight and came out bruised and best friends.*
     Score: 10 points

Meet Mr. Johnny Mathis . . .

My wife is a great singer, and I don't use the word lightly. Her favorite singer is Johnny Mathis, and I agree, the man sings like no one else. His staying power in a business where you are here today, gone tomorrow, is a record in itself. At this writing Johnny is appearing locally and Debbie called for reservations. Sold out two weeks ago. The man hasn't had a hit in years . . . but . . . who cares? Who can sing like Mathis?

Naturally, when he was in Houston while I was a "top jock" there, Debbie expected me to get us backstage. No problem. I knew the owner of the arena in which he was to perform that night. Debbie and I got there a little early . . . and . . . my friend, the owner was cleaning up the seats. (Being the owner is not all it's cracked up to be). I asked the question and got a quick response.

"Ron, I can't even get back there. He is still putting together the second show and it's only two hours from showtime. Sorry."

I knew this man was telling me the truth. No doubt about it. I also saw the look in Debbie's eyes. She had looked forward to this moment for weeks.

On came Mathis. The stage revolved so there was no bad seat. On one song, he just sat in the chair and sang with a lonely guitar accompanying him. I sat there and felt tears run down my face. I felt Debbie's hand clutch mine. I had never heard anyone, anywhere sing like that. Incredible. Intermission.

Don't ask me how I did it, but I got permission from Johnny's road manager to let us backstage for a few minutes. No, it wasn't a bribe. I just asked. I told her how important it was for Debbie. I told her that it was my wife's 30th birthday and this was the greatest present I could give her. I lied. But, I wasn't far off . . . and it worked.

We had five minutes.

"Ron, Debbie, meet Johnny Mathis." It was the manager. She left us alone in this room with "the king of necking music."

Me: "Johnny, this is my wife Debbie. I think she is your biggest fan."

Johnny: "Hello Debbie. It was nice of you two to come drop by."

He had changed clothes from a formal suit to a letter jacket, jeans, and tennis shoes. He couldn't have been any more relaxed nor more polite. He had a very pleasant manner and a constant smile. He seemed like he had all the time in the world.

Me: "I promised your manager that we would only take up a few minutes . . . I know this is your break time. Great show!"

Johnny: "Thanks. This is a fun place to play. The orchestra is excellent. I like the acoustics."

Debbie: "I loved that song with just the guitar and your voice."

Johnny: "That is a favorite of mine. It is always nice to just be there . . . just you and the guitar."

Me: "Do you have a favorite song of yours?

Johnny: (Laughs) "I guess it depends on the night, Ron. I love them all. I am proud of the newer material . . . people come to hear the older songs . . . I like them all."

Me: "You are so relaxed. So at ease. Does this ever get easy"?

Johnny: "I take every song and every job seriously, Ron. I don't guess I let it get easy. Oh yes, it is fun. I love it. It is a nice way to make a living. But, I suppose you could call me a perfectionist."

Debbie: "Ron and I . . . grew up on your music." (Smiles).

Johnny: (Laughs) "Make me feel old, eh"?

Debbie: "No, I didn't mean that . . . I meant . . . well, you've meant so much to us. To our relationship. Your music is very special and we will always . . . well Johnny . . . we will always love you for your music."

Me: "Mind if we take a few pictures. We'd better be going. I can't tell you how kind it was of you to take time out for us. We really appreciate it."

Johnny: "I appreciate your stopping by."

We took pictures. Debbie gave Johnny a big hug, I shook his hand. As he turned to walk away in his letter jacket, jeans, and tennis shoes, I was already getting ready for the second act. So was the audience. He got a five minute standing ovation.

Debbie Foster and her idol, Mr. Johnny Mathis.

(492) Q: What member of the Standells was once a Mousketeer?
A. *Paul Dodd*
B. *Dick Dodd*
C. *Dee Dodd*
D. *Dot Dodd*
Score: 10 points

(493) True or false? The Kinks took their name from the word "Kinky"?
Score: 5 points

Chance, Debbie, Mike Love from The Beach Boys, and Shawna.

Questions

(494) True or false? The Kinks created the distorted sound on their guitars in the hits "You Really Got Me" and "All Day and All of the Night" by turning their amplifiers up all the way and then kicking in the speakers?
Score: 5 points

(495) Q: Which Beatle song was recorded in an attempt to get their manager Brian Epstein out of a severe depression?
A. *"You Can't Do That"*
B. *"Baby, You're a Rich Man"*
C. *"Lady Madonna"*
D. *"Let It Be"*
Score: 7 points

(496) Q: What was the first #1 song of the rock era to use a synthesizer?
A. *"The Happy Organ"*
B. *"Runaway"*
C. *"Be My Baby"*
D. *"Rock Your Baby"*
Score: 7 points

(497) **Q: Who had the fifties version of "Blue Velvet"?**
A. *The Velvets*
B. *Bobby Vinton had the original in the sixties. Another trick question.*
C. *The Clovers*
D. *The Monotones*
Score: 10 points

(498) **Q: In 1955, who did Ed Sullivan ask to sing "16 Tons" on his really big show?**
A. *Tennesee Ernie Ford*
B. *Thomas Ernie Ford*
C. *Pat Boone*
D. *Bo Diddley*
Score: 10 points

Questions

(499) **Q: What was the filming budget for the movie "A Hard Day's Night"?**
A. *$1.25 million*
B. *$12.5 million*
C. *$2.25 million*
D. *$25 million*
Score: 9 points

(500) **Q: What did producer Phil Spector do to help insure airplay of the Righteous Brothers' "You've Lost That Livin' Feelin'"?**

Ron, John, and Pat. Pat and I were interviewing a coat hanger.

A. *He sent out Valentine chocolates in the shape of 45 rpm records to all major radio stations in the U.S.*
B. *He shortened the time on the label of the song..*
C. *He offered the Righteous Brothers for 10 free personal appearances and 2 concerts to the first 10 stations to play it.*
D. *He sent girls in bikinis to the stations to deliver the song.*
Score: 8 points

(501) Q: According to Keith Richards, what song was "Satisfaction" loosely based on?
A. "Twist and Shout"
B. "Dancin' in the Streets"
C. "Honky Tonkin'"
D. "Honky Tonk Parts I and II"
Score: 6 points

(502) Q: What was the first American record to sell a million copies during the onslaught of the British invasion from 1964-1967?
A. "One Fine Day"
B. "He's So Fine"
C. "Wooly Bully"
D. "She's About a Mover"
Score: 10 points

(503) Q: A TV series was planned around the "inspired lunacy" of the Beatles' "A Hard Day's Night." The Monkeys were assembled after exhausting auditions. What group, already established, was originally chosen to play the part of the group?
A. The Beatles
B. The Turtles
C. The Lovin' Spoonful
D. The Dave Clark Five

Score: 10 points

Find Ace Ventura.

Contact.

Questions

(504)   **Q: True or false? The Monkeys' first album came within less than about 10,000 records of outselling the Beatles' first LP?**
Score: 5 points

(505)   **Q: Who said: "My definition of soul is that inner feeling . . . it's a way of selling a song . . . projecting it and making it believable to the listener"?**
A. *Ray Charles*
B. *Stevie Wonder*
C. *Righteous Brother Bobby Hatfield*
D. *Joe Cocker*
Score: 8 points

(506)   **Q: What successful act of the sixties has built a career around the idea of "Taking Untouchable classic oldies and revitalizing them in his/her own style?**
A. *Linda Ronstadt*
B. *The Carpenters*
C. *Pat Boone*
D. *Johnny Rivers*
Score: 7 points

(507) Q: Bill Haley and the Comets went on a world tour in 1957. How many fans saw them?
A. *Over 500,000*
B. *About 100,000*
C. *Over a million*
D. *Bill Haley and the Comets never went on tour in Europe.*
Score: 7 points

(508) Q: The Beatles played their first concert at the Washington Coliseum in Washington DC. Who else was on the bill?
A. *Tommy Roe, The Chiffons and The Carvelles*
B. *The Shirelles, The Chiffons and Duane Eddy*
C. *A comedian named Bobby Vulgars*
D. *Bo Diddley and the Everly Brothers*
Score: 9 points

(509) Q: What was unusual about the Beatles' contract with Brian Epstein?
A. *The Beatles did not sign it.*
B. *Epstein did not sign it.*
C. *Neither the Beatles nor Epstein signed it.*
D. *It was handwritten on schoolbook paper.*
Score: 9 points

(510) Q: What were Jerry Lee Lewis's instructions from the Grand Ole Opry before his first appearance?
A. *No cussin' and no rock 'n' roll*
B. *No drums allowed on stage*
C. *No hip gyrations*
D. *No drinkin' and no cussin'*
Score: 9 points

(511) Q: Who holds the record for having the widest gaps between #1 singles?
A. *The Beatles*
B. *Paul Anka*
C. *Elvis*
D. *Johnny Rivers*
Score: 10 points

"Maybe I shouldn't ask, but why is your dress expanding?"

(512) Q: Because of protests by women's groups, what did Paul Anka do with "You're Havin' My Baby" while on tour?
A. *He fasted.*
B. *He didn't perform it.*
C. *He dropped the song.*
D. *He changed the words.*
Score: 6 points

(513) Q: Which group tried to name themselves "The Children of Howard Hughes" but ran into legal hassles?
A. *Huey Lewis and the News*
B. *The Hues Corporation*
C. *Sly and the Family Stone*
D. *The Flamingos*
Score: 7 points

Looks like fun to me.

(514) Q: As Voyager I speeds through the Galaxy it broadcasts greetings in many language-blips which can be decoded into black and white color images, and 90 minutes of music including one rock hit. Name that song.
A. *"Rock Around the Clock"*
B. *"Love Train"*
C. *"Johnny B. Goode"*
D. *"Good Vibrations"*
Score: 10 points

(515) Q: What is Chuck Berry's full real name?
A. *Charles Edward Berry*
B. *Chuck Van Berry*
C. *Charles Morrison Nelson Berry*
D. *Charles Edward Anderson Berry*
Score: 10 points

(516) Q: Which #1 song of the rock era written in response to the 1954 U.S. Supreme court decision banning segregation in public schools?
A. *"People Got To Be Free"*
B. *"Family Affair"*
C. *"Black and White"*
D. *"Love Train"*
Score: 10 points

(517) Q: Who gave the song "The First Time Ever I Saw Your Face" its big break?
A. *Robert Redford*
B. *Clint Eastwood*
C. *Richard Nixon*
D. *The Beach Boys*
Score: 6 points

(518) Q: What was the first song of the rock era to be #1 by two different artists?
A. *"Rock and Roll Music"*
B. *"The Locomotion"*
C. *"Go Away Little Girl"*
D. *"Don't Be Cruel"*
Score: 10 points

Questions

(519) Q: Who wrote James Taylor's "You've Got A Friend"?
A. *Carly Simon*
B. *James Taylor*
C. *Carole Kine*
D. *Tom Jones*
Score: 7 points

(520) Q: What was Anne Murray's biggest hit?
A. *"Snowbird"*
B. *"You Needed Me"*
C. *"You Can't Do That"*
D. *"Missing You"*
Score: 8 points

That's me on the left with my best buddy, Dennis. He once hit me on the head with a hammer thinking he was Roy Rogers. I had to have three stitches. The next week I "accidentally" put about 200 red ants on his back with a broom. That's what you get for growing up together across the street as best buddies. We went to college together and remain good friends. Forget Rollerblades. Ha. With these things we could make the block in less than an hour.

(521) Q: **What was the most successful rock oriented motion picture musical as of 1980?**
A. *"West Side Story"*
B. *"Rock, Rock, Rock"*
C. *"Grease"*
D. *"Urban Cowboy"*
Score: 9 points

(522) Q: **What was Paul McCartney's estimated financial net worth at the beginning of this decade?**
A. *$1 million*
B. *$10 million*
C. *$100 million*
D. *$1 billion*
Score: 9 points

Questions

(523) Q: **What was Johnny Mathis's only #1 song?**
A. *"Chances Are"*
B. *Johnny Mathis had 11 number one songs! Trick question*
C. *"Maria"*
D. *Johnny Mathis never had a #1 song.*
Score: 9 points

"Tom. Relax. You've been holding that record for 10 minutes."

(524) Q: **How did Daryl Hall and John Oates meet?**
A. *They grew up in the same neighborhood in Philadelphia and played together as kids.*
B. *They were seated next to each other on a flight which almost crashed on route from New York to Los Angeles.*
C. *They met as a result of a traffic accident in which Daryl came out bruised but best friends.*
D. *They met in an elevator while attempting to escape a fight between rival gangs at a record shop in Philadelphia.*
Score: 10 points

(525) Q: What mid-seventies vocal group evolved from the instrumental combo, the T-Bones?
A. *KC and the Sunshine Band*
B. *The Bay City Rollers*
C. *The Ohio Players*
D. *Hamilton, Joe Frank and Reynolds*
Score: 10 points

(526) Q: Elton John has a habit of making his songs collector's items. How did he accomplish this on "Philadelphia Freedom"?
A. *The back side of the record was signed by Paul McCartney.*
B. *He personally autographed every single.*
C. *He included a rare duet with John Lennon.*
D. *He included a rare duet with Mike Love.*
Score: 8 points

(527) Q: Which group was the first in rock history to be labeled "Symphonic" Rockers?
A. *The Beatles*
B. *The Moody Blues*
C. *The Rolling Stones*
D. *The Electric Light Orchestra*
Score: 10 points

"Now, turn on the machine that goes 'ping'."

(528) **Q: What particularly interesting thing happened when each Beatle received a "Member of the Order of the British Empire" award from the Queen in 1965?**
A. *Over 20,000 letters of congratulations came in a week.*
B. *The Beatles immediately increased their concert fee.*
C. *Many previous recipients mailed back their medals in protest.*
D. *The Beatles were asked to perform for the President of the Unites States-up until then they had been shunned.*
Score: 8 points

(529) **Q: Phil Spector produced many hits by many groups throughout the years . . . from "To Know Him Is To Love Him" by the Teddybears to "Let It Be" by the Beatles. What song is considered to be his greatest achievement as a producer?**
A. *"Let It Be" – the album*
B. *"Be My Baby"*
C. *"You've Lost that Lovin' Feelin'"*
D. *"Unchained Melody"*
Score: 8 points

Page 154

Questions

(530) **Q: Who was first called "The King" of rock 'n' roll?**
A. *Blues singer, Muddy Waters*
B. *Elvis*
C. *Bill Haley*
D. *Chuck Berry*
Score: 8 points

(531) **Q: What was the first song Bill Haley put on the charts?**
A. *"Crazy Man, Crazy"*
B. *"Rock, Rock, Rock"*
C. *"Rockin' Man"*
D. *"Rock Around the Clock"*
Score: 8 points

(532) **Q: In what year was Fats Domino at his peak chartwise?**
A. *1956*
B. *1957*
C. *1958*
D. *1959*
Score: 10 points

Believe it or not, this man actually went on to become a professional fashion designer.

(533) **Q: How many songs did Fats Domino put on the charts from 1955 to 1959?**
A. *33*
B. *44*
C. *Almost 50*
D. *Almost 70*

Note: The correct answer depends on the source and includes all charted songs, not necessarily big hits. Remember that many of his songs were double-sided hits although only one side may have charted. Now that I've given away the answer . . .
Score: 3 points

(534) **Q: Jerry Fuller wrote "Travelin' Man" and produced a demo using Glen Campbell and Dave Burgess of the Champs as backup. The song was written and the demo was made for whom?**
A. *Elvis*
B. *Gene Pitney*
C. *Rickey Nelson*
D. *Sam Cooke*
Score: 10 points

(535) **Q: Name at least five acts that Phil Spector produced?**
Score: 2 points each (Answers on next page)

(536) **Q: What started Dean Martin's "Second Career"?**
A. *His appearance on the Jerry Lewis Labor Day Telethon*
B. *His role in "The Kentuckian"*
C. *The song "Everybody Loves Somebody Sometime"*
D. *The song "That's Amoré"*
Score: 10 points

(537) **Q: When "Everybody Loves Somebody" went all the way to #1 right in the middle of the British invasion, Dean Martin called Elvis with what has become a classic line in Rock 'n' Roll history. What's that line?**
A. *"Well, if you can't handle the Beatles, I can."*
B. *"Next time I get first billing."*
C. *"Hello, may I speak to Elvis what's-his-name"?*
D. *"Move over Big E, I knocked out the Big B, here comes the Big D"*
Score: 10 points

(538) Q: What British group was considered the most "Intense"?
A. *The Kinks*
B. *The Rolling Stones*
C. *The Dave Clark Five*
D. *The Doors*
Score: 10 points

(539) Q: Who did Elvis once introduce as "one of the greatest singers in the world"?
A. *Little Richard*
B. *Pat Boone*
C. *Johnny Mathis*
D. *Roy Orbison*
Score: 10 points

(540) Q: Shirley Owens was the lead singer of the Shirelles. True or False? The group names themselves after her.
Score: 9 points

Questions

Answer from previous page: Among others, Phil Spector produced the Crystals, the Righteous Brothers, Bob B. Soxx and the Blue Jeans, the Drifters, Gene Pitney, Ike and Tina Turner and the Beatles. He also sang along with the Teddybears on "To Know Him Is to Love Him" which counts too. Also, if you guessed the Blossoms, give yourself another 10 points! They are the group that actually sang the song "He's a Rebel" although the Crystals got credit on the label. Darlene Love, their lead singer played Danny Glover's wife in the "Lethal Weapon" movies.

(541) Q: "Calcutta" by Lawrence Welk
went to #1 on the pop charts–
How high did it get on the soul
charts?

A. *What a ridiculous trick question. It didn't
make the soul charts. Give me a break.*
B. *It hit #100 on what is considered a mis-
take or fluke.*
C. *The song made the top 10.*
D. *It went all the way to #1.*
Score: 8 points

"Honey. Remember that term paper of yours
I lost that kept you out of med. school?
Guess what?"

(542) Q: In what year did Chubby
Checker star in the "B" Japanese
movie, "It's Atomic . . . The
Twister"?

A. *1964*
B. *1965*
C. *1960*
D. *This is another stupid trick question*
Score: 8 points

(543) Q: How many copies of the Supremes' 1st single were sold internationally?

A. *Almost 20 million*
B. *Just under 1 million*
C. *Over 500,000*
D. *Less than 100*
Score: 10 points

(544) True or False? Chubby Checker once starred in a movie entitled
"Don't Knock The Twist"?
Score: 5 points

(545) Q: What was the original name of Herman's Hermits?

A. *Herman and the Hermits*
B. *The Heartbeats*
C. *Herman's Hermits*
D. *The British Hermits*
Score: 10 points

(545) Q: Did Elvis sign up for the Army or was he drafted?
Score: 5 points

(547) Q: Elvis made a comeback special for NBC on December 1, 1968. What did he do as he left the stage?
A. *Signed autographs*
B. *Collapsed*
C. *Split his pants*
D. *Walked back for an encore*
Score: 9 points

(548) Q: What were Sam's and Dave's last names?
A. *Moore and Prater*
B. *Jones and Prater*
C. *Smith and Jones*
D. *Moore and Jenkins*
Score: 9 points

(549) Q: Name the first artists of the rock era to have their first three singles released go to #1.
A. *Simon and Garfunkle*
B. *The Everly Brothers*
C. *The Jackson Five*
D. *Abba*
Score: 9 points

Questions

Shawna, Bruce Johnston, Debbie, and Chance before a recent Beach Boys concert.

(550)　Q: Where was Ringo when the Beatles began recording "Hey Jude" – the real session which was eventually released?
A. *In the men's room*
B. *In his car sleeping*
C. *Asleep in the drum booth*
D. *Making out under a studio piano*
Score: 9 points

(551)　Q: What famous singer of the sixties began his career at the age of 16 by joining "The Bimbo Show"?
A. *This is a trick question*
B. *Bobby Lewis*
C. *Gary Lewis*
D. *Ringo Starr*
Score: 10 points

Can we really keep these?

Questions

(552)　Q: Who grabbed a hunk of his hair and tossed it at reporters with this classic line: "Hair Today, Gone Tomorrow"?
A. *A balding Bobby Vee*
B. *Elvis*
C. *Paul after his Beatle days*
D. *James Taylor when he noticed his hair was falling out*
Score: 7 points

(553)　True or false? Buddy Holly was more popular in Britain than he was in America in his early days?
Score: 5 points

(554)　Q: What is considered as the first heavy metal instrumental?
A. *"Frankenstein"*
B. *"Last Night"*
C. *"Rumble"*
D. *"Sleepwalk"*
Score: 10 points

(555) Q: Name all the words to "Louie, Louie."

For many years our little devious minds have conjured up all kinds of absurd lyrics to words we can't understand. After once giving some of the lyrics over the air I have had calls from band members who are still singing the song after all these years and I hear things like . . . "Are you sure?" I'm Sure!

Richard Berry* had the original. All you have to do is listen closely to his version and hear the actual words to the classic hit. Next time you hear us play it, sing along . . . and bring the kids.

> "Louie Louie me gotta go. Louie Louie me gotta go.
> (To work I go).
> A fine little girl she waits for me. Me catch a ship
> across the sea. I sail the ship all alone. Me never think
> me make it home.
>
> *Repeat chorus*
>
> Lonely nights and days we sailed the sea. Me think of
> girls constantly. On the ship I dream she's there. I
> smell the rose in her hair.
>
> *Repeat chorus*
>
> I see Jamaican moon above. It won't be long me see
> me love. Me take her in my arms again and then I tell
> her I never leave again."
>
> *Repeat chorus*
>
> ***100 points if you got all the words right.***

*Words and music © by Richard Berry

Trivia Answers

Trivia Answers

1. C. There really is a Dead Man's Curve near U.C.L.A. in L.A. The famous voice of Buggs Bunny, Tweetie, Sylvester-Mel Blanc-once had a near fatal wreck there which eventually became the inspiration for the song.

2. A. Elvis. Surprisingly, Dorsey Burnette also graduated from the same high school at about the same time.

3. D. Richard Berry wrote it and was the first to record it. Paul Revere and the Raiders did take a shot at it, but it was the Kingsmen's version which became the classic partly due to the fact that the words were hard to understand. There has circulated for years a rumor that the drummer dropped a stick while the song was being recorded and yelled out a profane word which can easily be heard on the song . . . if you listen for it . . . and even then it's subjective.

4. False. According to my interview with Roger McGuinn, lead singer of the Byrds and the one who wore the square glasses, Glen Campbell did not show up for the session and thus, despite the information given in many reputable trivia books, was not present.

5. C. The very audible clink near the end of the recording is actually Jerry Lee Lewis dropping a nickel in a soda machine. It can be heard near the very end of the song.

6. B.

7. D. During the interview I asked him when was the last time he was on Mars and he hesitated, laughed, and said he went there and got back WHILE I WAS ASKING THE QUESTION. I waver from believing he is saying it for some sort of publicity to actually believing he actually believes it.

8. C. Carole King co-wrote the song and asked if she might play the kettle drums. They are very difficult to hear unless you have a good set of earphones and a CD version of the song.

9. C. This one gets 'em every time. "I'll Cry Instead" has a definite country sound and was the first record to be recognized by critics as country sounding.

10. C. Can you believe that? This answer came from Dion himself.

11. B. "My Sweet Lord" makes me feel like I'm walking through an airport.

12. D. The Beach Boys' version was a little too slow and disjointed,

but was a good rendition of the song. The Hondells speeded it up; their harmony resembles that of the Beach Boys.

13. A.

14. D. The label indicates the Crystals sang the song, but in reality the Blossoms actually voiced it. As the story goes the Crystals were on tour – out of town at least – and Phil Spector heard that Vicki Lawrence had already recorded the song and was about to release it. Feeling it was hit material Phil called in the studio group, the Blossoms. Because the Crystals were the most established group, their name appears on the label. Darlene Love, lead singer plays Danny Glover's wife in the "Lethal Weapon" series.

15. B.

16. A.

17. A.

18. B.

19. A.

20. C. Dean was one-half of Jan and Dean. Brian Wilson worked closely with them on several of their hits including their biggest, "Surf City." I hosted a 1994 concert with Jan and Dean in Arkansas.

21. C.

22. C.

23. D.

24. B.

25. C.

26. D. From the book of Ecclesiastes in the Old Testament between Proverbs and the Psalms. If you want to look it up go to Chapter 3 beginning with the first verse. In the Bible the words "I swear" are not used. It is a very interesting text.

27. B.

28. A.

29. A.

30. B. One listen to the words and the answer to this question is obvious.

31. D.

32. C. I have had the privilege to work with Ronnie Milsap and he is quite amazing. Ronnie is blind, but when he sits on top of the piano Jerry-Lee-Lewis style at a concert, you would never know it. Ronnie is an inspiration.

33. A.

34. C.

35. D.

36. A.

37. C.

38. A. The Elegants' "Little Star" was such a hit that they were immediately called to go on an extensive tour. They did. By the time they got back, they had lost momentum at home and were never able to gain it back.

39. A. His real name was Harold Lloyd Jenkins. The Conway Twitty came from a town in Texas and in Arkansas-Conway-Twitty. Neat way to pick a name.

40. A.

41. D.

42. C. Believe it or not! Pat sold more records that year than Elvis especially considering the immense success of "Love Letters In The Sand" which topped the charts for 7 weeks and was on the charts for 34.

43. C. Yes, 10 years. Another incredible record for Johnny Mathis.

44. A. When the Everly Brothers appeared on the Grand Ole Opry they were not allowed to have their drummer seen on stage. These are the same rocket scientists who told Elvis that he should go back to driving a truck.

45. A.

46. C. It can clearly be heard off a CD stereo version of the song.

47. C.

48. C. They said it was "too violent" and that "blood ran in the grooves."

49. C.

50. D.

51. B. In those days rock 'n' roll was not a given. Would it last? No one knew. Not even Elvis. So, the idea was that they had been lucky on their first song and they had better get back on track and be safe for their second. Their follow up song was actually a protest against the record company – "Rock and Roll is Here to Stay."

52. C.

53. B.

54. C.

55. B.

56. D.

57. B.

58. B.

59. B. The nickname was made in good humor as a reference to the beginning of his biggest hit "Summertime" in which he starts off . . . well . . . as a motormouth.

60. A.

61. A. The two versions released, one by the Shadows of Knight and the other by Them were both hits.

62. B.

63. A.

64. B.

65. B.

66. B.

67. B. He also cleaned ashtrays at a record company. His hit "I Can Help" was a worldwide smash.

68. C. It was actually recorded in their front yard during a block party sort of thing.

69. C. He was originally Billy Joe Thomas but after the success of Billy Joe Royal, B. J. did not want to confuse matters, thus the initials.

70. B. This guy is for real.

71. A.

72. B. Hank Ballard had this hit. One of the lines begins with: "There's a thrill upon the hill, let's go, let's go, let's go."

73. B.

74. B. Paul made a mistake on the song as he had Desmond putting on his pretty make up rather than Molly. After the recording Paul told the guys he had made the mistake and suggested the song be cut over. The others hadn't heard it and only after a playback did they begin to laugh and encourage Paul to leave it as it was. Paul agreed saying: "People will wonder what kind of guy Desmond is."

75. C. They had several hits but nothing like the Coaster days. One Robins' hit I particularly think you would enjoy is "Smokey Joe's Cafe" – a classic!

76. A.

77. A.

78. C. His version did receive some airplay, but was not a major hit . . . at least enough of a hit to cause a national twist craze. Chubby Checker was called in by Dick Clark because Chubby was known for his impersonations. He was trying to sound like Hank Ballard when he recorded the song and did. Hank heard it on the radio years after his initial release and thought it was his original version! It seems like Chubby gets all the credit for the song when Hank Ballard actually wrote it and recorded it first . . . however, since Hank did write it, he gets the writer's fee or residual which over the years had been very substantial.

79. C. The hit was "Telstar"

80. A.

81. A and B. Give yourself 5 points for either you got correct. Subtract 5 from each you got wrong.

82. B.

83. C. They tried, but with no success . . . they just couldn't make it happen.

84. C.

85. A.

86. D. Remember the Supremes did not come along until about the mid sixties.

87. True

88. B.

89. D.

90. D.

91. C.

92. B.

93. C.

94. C.

95. D.

96. B.

97. B. Ron Foster at age 11. If you guessed George Bush, deduct 10 points. Good grief!!

98. B. By Connie Francis

99. C.

100. C.

101. B.

102. B.

103. C.

104. C. They tried a number of different names and sounds and did not hit it big until they copied the style of Maurice Williams and the Zodiacs.

105. C.

106. A.

107. C.

108. D.

109. C.

110. B.

111. A.

112. B. Listen to the two songs back to back and you can hear his distinct style.

113. B.

114. C.

115. A.

116. D.

117. C.

118. D.

119. B.

120. B.

121. False – he was about 30

122. B.

123. A.

124. A. He is certainly the founding father of rock. Some consider him The King. I wouldn't argue.

125. C. They had their own hit with "Don't Say Nothin' Bad About My Baby".

126. D. It was Bruce Channel's harmonica player, Delbert McClinton who caught John Lennon's attention on "Hey Baby." Delbert taught John how to play the harmonica.

127. B.

128. B.

129. False. The Peppermint Lounge

130. D.

Answers

Answers

131. D. Brian Wilson has only partial hearing in one ear and thus did not notice or care whether the song was recorded in mono.

132. C.

133. C.

134. D.

135. A.

136. B.

137. A.

138. A.

139. B.

140. D.

141. B.

142. D.

143. B.

144. C. Most of the versions of the song which are not sold in America now contain the Ringo version.

145. C.

146. B. A song he wrote while observing his wife walk out the door on her way to go grocery shopping.

147. C.

148. A.

149. C.

150. A. (If you guessed Link Ray and "Rumble" go ahead and give yourself 10 points – a case could be made for either answer).

151. B.

152. A.

153. A.

154. C. Ringo was quoted as saying: "There were all the other songs and then their was 'Rain.' I did my best drumming on that one and it is my favorite of all our songs."

155. C.

156. D.

157. C.

158. C.

159. A. Herb Alpert played all the instruments himself on that early recording.

160. C.

161. A.

162. C.

163. D.

164. B.

165. A.

166. C.

167. C.

168. B.

169. C.

170. B.

171. D. In 1949

172. C.

173. A.

174. A.

175. D.

176. A.

177. B.

178. C.

179. A.

180. D.

181. A.

182. C.

183. A.

184. C.

185. A.

186. C.

187. B.

188. C.

189. A. One officially kicked off the rock era and the other signalled the British Invasion.

190. The Byrds by about 2 weeks

191. D.

192. B.

193. A.

194. C.

195. A.

196. B.

197. D.

198. A, B, and C. Count each correct answer as 5 points for a possible total of not 10 but a bonus 15. (Author's note: It is my opinion that we are so near the Biblical end times, it may be a whole new world in 2525).

199. A.

200. B.

201. C.

202. A.

203. True

204. D.

205. B.

206. B. Brian Wilson said that the word surfin' was his word for freedom.

207. C. What do critics know anyway and where do they get their "Critic" degrees?

208. D. He invented the sewing maching as you probably well know, so why did they dedicate the movie to him? For the heck of it – to be different – so we would be asking trivia questions about it years later.

209. B.

210. B.

211. D. Del was in England when he recognized the potential of the Beatles as a group and the song "From Me To You" in particular. He asked John if he could record it and was told yes. Later, John had second thoughts and asked Del not to release it in the U.S. However, Del did and had a small hit with the song! Del was actually having Beatle hits in America before the Beatles.

212. B. Of the same name.

213. A.

214. C.

215. C.

216. B.

217. C.

218. D.

219. D.

220. D.

221. D.

222. B.

223. C.

224. D.

225. D.

226. C.

227. B.

228. A.

229. C.

230. A.

231. C. He went on to record "Be-Bop-A-Lula" which was a big hit for him. His success was limited after that initial recording.

232. 25 points – Jerry Lee Lewis

233. "Tammy"

234. "I Just Don't Understand"

235. C.

236. B.

237. C.

238. C.

239. B.

240. B.

241. C. One of the original Million Dollar Singers along with Elvis, Carl Perkins and Jerry Lee Lewis. Rufus Thomas also first recorded on Sun.

242. B.

243. A. For a girl named . . . you got it . . . Donna.

244. D.

245. B. They thought the song was so goofy-stupid-different that you can actually hear the lead singer laugh on the recording which eventually made it to vinyl.

246. D.

247-273. Every answer contained in the Special Elvis Bonus Section is TRUE

274. A.

275. D. He debuted the song on "The Ozzie and Harriet Show"

276. C.

277. B.

278. D.

279. D.

280. A. They were from Texas and were a very successful attempt to cash in on the popularity of British groups

281. B.

282. C.

283. C. It was meant as a joke.

284. D.

285. A.

286. D.

287. D.

288. C.

289. D.

290. A.

291. C.

292. C.

293. C.

294. D.

295. D.

296. B.

297. C.

298. False

299. True

300. C.

301. B.

302. B.

303. D.

304. C.

305. C.

306. B.

307. True

308. True

309. A.

310. D.

311. B. I have heard the original which is quite similar to the Tokens' version.

312. B. Bobby went from radio station to radio station with roses to promote "Roses Are Red". It worked.

313. A.

314. A.

315. C. A lawsuit came about which resulted in the author of the song being listed as Chuck Berry.

316. D.

317. D.

318. D.

319. C.

320. True

321. C. Jeff Barry and Ellie Greenwich

322. C.

323. C. This is generally accepted as his favorite. "It's Now or Never" also gets mentioned so if that was your choice, go ahead and give yourself those additional five points.

324. B.

325. C.

326. D. Brian Wilson's mom used to tell him this . . . about vibrations. When you think about it, it certainly makes sense.

327. C.

328. C.

329. A.

330. A.

331. D.

332. B.

333. D.

334. C.

335. If you were the 1st to notice their is no question # 335, give yourself 25 points.

336. B.

337. D.

338. C.

339. B. (Internationally)

340. A.

341. There is no question 341. If you were the first to notice, give yourself 15 points

342. A.

343. C.

344. C.

345. D.

346. D. I disagree with the King on this one.

347. A.

348. C.

349. B.

350. B.

351. B.

352. B. It was a complete flop.

353. B.

354. True

355. D.

356. A.

357. A.

358. C.

359. B.

360. C.

361. A and B – Otis and Sam. 10 points for each or a total of 20 points.

362. B.

363. C.

364. B.

365. D. Phil also sang on that song however it is not the first song he produced.

366. B and C – Mickey and Davy.

367. D.

368. Answers on page 111.

369. B.

370. B.

371. C. The Colonel wanted $5,000 for an Elvis appearance . . .

372. C. And the union scale was $138

373. B.

374. B.

375. B. The ratings were down and the kids were not dancing. "Quarter to Three" put the life back

into the dancers and eventually the ratings. This was a critical moment in rock and roll history. One has to ask what would have happened if "American Banstand" had been cancelled.

376. D. It worked. It was his first hit.

377. C.

378. B.

379. C.

380. B.

381. D. Dick Clark is one of the really nice guys in this business. His net worth well exceeds that mark today.

382. B.

383. B. Some sources list "Think" as reaching #1 so we will give you 6 points for answering A.

384. Answers on page 115

385. C.

386. D.

387. B.

388. There is no question 388. Give yourself 15 points if you were the first to notice. Yo mama!

389. C.

390. B.

391. D. "Met her at a dance lookin' for romance . . ."

392. C.

393. D.

394. D.

395. D.

396. C.

397. C.

398. D.

399. C.

400. C.

401. B.

402. D.

403. B.

404. B.

405. A.

406. D.

407. D.

408. D.

409. A.

410. D. Think about it.

411. C.

412. A.

413. B.

414. B. Because Jesse Garon was stillborn was probably the main reason Gladys became overly protective of Elvis. He was nicknamed "Mama's Boy" because she used to walk him to school each day. Elvis and his mother were very close.

415. D.

416. B.

Answers

417. C. It was called "My Girl Sloopy."

418. A.

419. A.

420. C. After his hit "Tiptoe Through the Tulips"

421. B.

422. C.

423. D.

424. C.

425. D.

426. C.

427. D.

428. C.

429. C.

430. D.

431. C.

432. A.

433. C.

434. B.

435. B.

436. B.

437. C.

438. C.

439. C.

440. D.

441. A.

442. B.

443. D.

444. C.

445. D.

446. D.

447. C.

448. D.

449. C.

450. A.

451. B.

452. C.

453. D.

454. C.

455. C.

456. D.

457. B.

458. A.

459. C.

460. A.

461. C.

462. B.

463. A.

464. C.

465. D. Yep, Fats!

466. Shelly, Lincoln, Arnold, Bob, Fred, Mary, Bo, Tony, Mony, Billy, Marsha, Nick.

467. C.

468. C.

469. B.

470. B.

471. B.

472. A.

473. B.

474. C.

475. A.

476. True.

477. C.

478. A.

479. A.

480. B.

481. A.

482. A.

483, 484. Answers on page 141

486. A.

487. A.

488. True.

489. True.

490. A.

491. D.

492. B.

493. True.

494. False. There are several versions of basically the same story. The most probable version has the group attempting the song over and over only winding up totally frustrated with the sound. While they were on a break their producer simply sliced the speakers in their amplifiers resulting in the distortion which became their early trademark.

495. B. They thought that letting him know in song just how much money he had would bring him out. In this case, money did not buy happiness.

496. B.

497. C.

498. D. He sang "Bo Diddley" instead. Way to go Bo!

499. A.

500. B. Radio stations were reluctant to play songs over 3 minutes in length. The song's label had it coming in near the 3 minute mark when actually it was over 3 minutes and 30 seconds.

501. C. By Hank Williams

502. C.

503. C. The producers realized that they would have more control over a new group in that the "Spoonful" were already established and more or less independent.

504. False. It outsold the Beatles!

505. C.

506. D. "Memphis," "Midnight Special," "Baby, I Need Your Lovin'." Johnny's only number one song incidentally was "Poor Side of Town" and he wrote that one.

507. A.

508. A.

509. B.

510. A. And he did both.

511. B. "Diana" in 1957 and "You're Havin' My Baby" in 1974 – 15 years and 2 weeks apart

512. D. He changed "my" to "our" baby. Takes two to tango Paul.

513. B.

514. C.

515. D.

516. C.

517. B. Eastwood personally asked Roberta Flack if she would allow the song to be used in "Play Misty for Me." She agreed. It had been released earlier and had not been a hit.

518. C. Steve Lawrence and Donny Osmond.

519. A.

520. B.

521. C.

522. D.

523. A.

524. D.

525. D.

526. C.

527. B.

528. C. Ironically, the Beatles later returned their medals in a kind of counterprotest.

529. C.

530. C. Haley was 30 years old when "Rock Around the Clock" hit the charts. He eventually became what many consider to be a recluse, allegedly drank heavily, and died of a heart attack.

531. A.

532. The correct answer is A, B, C, or D. All answers win. See next question for reason. You can't lose with Captain Trivia.

533. D.

534. D. His manager turned it down.

535. Answers on page 156.

536. C.

537. A.

538. C. Another word for loud.

539. D.

540. False. They said they chose the name "because it had a ring to it." But I'll bet Shirley didn't argue.

541. C. No, you are not seeing things. The top 10! This is why you have me here to help you with all this stuff. Who would have ever guessed this one?

542. D.

543. D. Their first "single" was not a "hit single."

544. True.

545. All answers could be right. Credible sources indicate that there

really were no Hermits – officially anyway. Just Herman and some studio musicians. Other sources seem to indicate a group consisting of Herman and the Hermits. It is also recorded that at one time Herman played in a group called the Heartbeats. A, B, C, and D could be right. Another bonus question. *Also, give yourself 50 points if you saw two question 545s. The answer to the Elvis question is that he was drafted. Everyone still has a chance to win don't they?*

547. B.

548. B.

549. C. There is a trick to the question. The Supremes had five number one songs in a row, but their first three <u>releases</u> were not number one.

550. A. He heard the song start without him and arrived at his drums just in time.

551. B. Of "Tossin' and Turnin'" fame.

552. B. As he got the Army haircut

553. False.

554. C. By Link Wray

Page 177

Answers

Index

A

Aaron, Hank 121

Aaron, Jesse 121

Abba 158

Akins, Jewel 118

Allen, Rex 43

Allen, Steve 113

Alpert, Herb 43

Anderson, Kerby 91

Angel, Mad 114

Angels, The 8

Animals, The 41, 137

Anka, Paul 13, 54, 68, 120, 127-128, 139-141, 149-150

Anka, Paula 37

Anthony, Eric 52

Anthony, Little 43

Archies, The 43

Argyles, The Hollywood 9, 141

Atkins, Chet 60, 63

Avalon, Frankie 10-11, 29, 67, 112, 127

Axton, Hoyt 60, 78

Axton, Mabel 60

B

Ballard, Hank 18-19, 120, 122

Balox, Buddy 15

Bandstand, American 10-12, 81, 110-112, 137-138

Barry, Len 54

Beatles, The 2, 18, 20, 25, 34, 36, 53, 57-59, 62, 64, 78-79, 84, 86-89, 94, 98, 103, 106, 110, 118, 121-122, 134, 140-141, 147-149, 153-156, 159

Beatles, The Silver 141

Beats, Rocco and the 67

Beatty, Warren 22

Bell, Archie 18, 98

Bellnotes, The 117

Belmonts, The 81, 112

Belushi, John 59

Berry, Chuck 2, 32, 60, 64, 67, 78, 150, 154

Berry, Richard 1, 160

Best, Pete 34, 39

Bidwell, David 15

Black, Bill 127

Blaine, Hal 2, 39

Blaine, Marcie 120

Bland, Billy 14

Bland, Bobby 14, 67

Bloom, Bobby 133

Blossoms, The 4, 156

Blues, The Moody 153

Bogart, Humphrey 66

Bono, Sonny 9, 29, 38, 62, 70, 100, 114, 127

Booker T. and the M.G.'s 109

Boone, Pat 4, 6, 10, 28-29, 31, 38, 40, 42, 48, 68, 79, 85, 111, 146, 148, 156

Bopper, Big 15, 19, 79, 100

Bopper, The Big 15, 19, 79, 100

Boyce, Tommy 13

Boys, The Beach 3, 5, 21, 27, 37, 49, 57, 82, 90, 94, 96-97, 113, 116, 122, 126, 145, 151

Brando, Marlon 56

Brass, Tijuana 43

Breakers, The Heart 89

Brennah, Edward E. 9

Brothers, Everly 10, 40, 57, 62, 82, 90, 93, 99, 112, 149, 158

Brothers, Righteous 57, 112, 146, 156

Brothers, The Everly 10, 40, 57, 62, 82, 90, 93, 99, 112, 149, 158

Brothers, The Righteous 112, 146, 156

Brothers, The Smothers 36

Brown, Charlie 69, 112, 132

Brown, James 43, 58, 83

Burdon, Eric 137

Burgess, Dave 155

Burnette, Dorsey 1

Burnette, Johnny 65

Bush, George 23

Byrds, The 13, 53, 137, 139

C

Cale, Michael 15

Campbell, Glen 1-2, 13, 60, 79, 81, 98, 114, 121, 155

Campbell, Glenn 47

Candea, Rick 50

Cannon, Freddie 31, 107

Carson, Johnny 90

Carter, Jimmy 30

Cash, Johnny 68

Castro, Fidel 5

Chaffee, Roger B. 24

Champs, The 155

Chandler, Gene 69, 119, 135

Channel, Bruce 36

Charles, Ray 8, 107, 148

Checker, Chubby 6, 10, 17-19, 37, 109, 120, 122, 157

Cher 29, 37, 81, 93, 139

Chiffons, The 4, 34, 57, 101, 109, 120, 149

Chordettes, The 11

Christie, Lou 54, 92

Clapton, Eric 47

Clark, Dick 10, 19, 70, 107, 110, 112-113, 126-127, 129

Clark, Petula 46, 102

Clarke, Pat 18, 47, 137

Clearwater, Creedance 83

Clovers, The 102, 117, 146

Coasters, The 18, 32, 77, 112

Cochran, Eddie 65, 68, 107, 140

Collins, Judy 54

Combo, Alan Price 41

Como, Perry 79

Conley, Arthur 108, 122

Cook, Don 109

Cook, John 15

Cooke, Sam 60, 108, 155

Cookies, The 34, 49, 101, 126

Cream 83

Crescents, The 134

Crofts, Seals and 123

Crosby, Bing 66

Crystals, The 4, 156

Cups, The Dixie 8, 119

Curtis, Tony 69

Cuts, The Crew 113

D

Daisley, Robert 15

Dance, The Circle 125

Darin, Babby 136

Darin, Bobby 11, 90, 125, 129

Darren, James 10

Davis, Bette 66

Davis, Sammy 124

Dead Man's Curve 1, 99, 108

Dean, James 29, 56, 66

Dean, Jan 5

Dean, Jan and 27, 64

Denver, John 89

Detours, The 94, 103-106

Diamond, Neil 92

Diamonds, The 11, 18-19, 32

Diddley, Bo 6, 42, 47, 60, 127, 146, 149

Diddly, Bo 101

Diddy, Do Wah Diddy 91

Dimension, The Fifth 43, 116

Dion 2, 4, 13, 38, 42, 56, 81, 100, 138

Dixon, Billy 52

Doe, Ernie K. 19, 45, 102

Dolenz, Mickey 109

Domino, Fats 11, 48, 111, 136, 154-155

Doors, The 156

Dorset, Ray 15

Dorsey Brother's Stage Show 113

Dowes, Charles Gates 9

Drifters, Clyde McPhatter and the 102

Drifters, The 80, 102, 156

Duke, The 47, 135

Dwight, Reginald Kenneth 18

Dyke, Dick Van 59

Dylan, Bob 13, 15, 31, 39, 44-45, 63, 68, 85, 110, 135

Index

E

Earl, Colin 15
Earl, Duke of 119, 135
Eastwood, Clint 151
Elegants, The 9, 141
Ellis, Shirley 22
Epstein, Brian 20, 57, 145, 149
Esptein, Brian 134
Eva, Little 2, 34, 126
Evans, Zager and 55, 141
Everlys, The Four 141

F

Fabares, Shelley 68
Fabares, Shelly 102, 135
Fabian 10, 29
Fawcett, Farrah 30
Festival, Woodstock 63
Fineley, Andrea 68
Five, The Dave Clark 136, 147, 156
Five, The Jackson 158
Fives, Dave Clark 91
Flamingos, The 31, 150
Floyd, Eddie 117
Ford, Gerald 9
Ford, Tennesee Ernie 146
Ford, Thomas Ernie 146
Foreman, George 32

Foster, Debbie 91, 144
Foster, Ron 2-3, 8, 23, 30, 37, 62, 90-91, 94, 102, 120, 125, 127, 139
Foundations, The 43
Francis, Connie 39, 81, 121
Fuller, Jerry 155
Funicello, Annette 68, 84

G

Gable, Clark 1, 52, 124
Garfunkle, Art 122
Garfunkle, Simon and 10, 85, 93, 112, 158
Garon, Jesse 121
Garr, Arty 122
Garrett, Snuff 139
Gates, David 13, 62-63
Gaye, Marvin 4, 6, 11, 27, 39-40, 108, 110, 138
Gees, The Bee 137
Generation, Sound 129
Gilley, Mickey 65
Glen, John 132
Glenn, Darrell 43
Goldboro, Bobby 109
Goldsboro, Bobby 98, 109
Goldwater, Barry 30
Goode, Johnny B. 78, 90, 125, 150
Gore, Leslie 27, 39

Goulet, Robert 28

Graceland 16, 56, 74, 137

Greenbaum, Norman 15, 141

Grissom, Virgil I. 24

Guidio, Bob 101

H

Haley, Bill 34, 38, 115, 140, 149, 154

Hall, Daryl 152

Hamilton, Ricky 106

Happenings, The 101

Harding, Tonya 55

Hardy, Laurel and 112

Hardy, Oliver 56

Harrison, George 3, 20, 69, 93, 117

Harrison, Paul 134

Hart, Bobby 13

Hawkin, Dale 125-126

Hendrix, Jimi 47-48, 60, 83

Hepburn, Katherine 124

Hi Fi's 43

Highwaymen, The 13

Hilderbrand, Ray 28

Hinton, Danny 15

Hodges, Eddie 132

Holly, Buddy 34, 38-39, 45, 64, 77, 79, 100, 118, 159

Hooch, Captain 52, 67

Hop, The Bunny 125

Horton, Johnny 46, 48

Howe, Elias 57

Huber, Heather 62

Humperdinck, Englebert 120

Hunter, Ivory Joe 79

Hunter, Steve 103, 106

I

Iglesias, Julio 22

Innocents, Kathy Young and the 8

Innocents, The 8, 65, 134

Inspirations, The Sweet 8, 34, 57

J

Jackson, Michael 111

Jagger, Mick 82, 134, 136

James, Sonny 55

James, Tommy 8, 45, 102

Jardine, Al 97

Jeans, Bob B. Soxx and the Blue 156

Jennings, Waylon 100

Jerry, Mungo 15, 141

Jesters, The Four 6

Jimmy D'Angelo 114

Jitterbug, The 125

Jo D'Angelo 114

John, Elton 11, 18, 63, 93, 98, 153

Index

John, Olivia Newton 15, 102

Johnston, Bruce 90, 121, 158

Jolson, Al 107

Jones, Davy 14, 109

Jones, George 2, 19, 79

Jones, Jimmy 118

Jones, Mike 136

Jones, Paul 136

Jones, Quincy 27

Jones, Tom 17, 151

Joneses, The 114

Joplin, Janice 134

Juniors, Danny and the 11-12, 19, 32, 52, 81, 122

K

Kendricks, Eddie 141

Kennedy, Cape 24

Kine, Carole 151

King, Carole 2, 40, 126, 135

King, Paul 15

Kingsmen 1, 36

Kingsmen, The 1, 36

Kinks, The 22, 145, 156

Klein, Carole 135

Knight, Gladys 27, 110, 134

Knox, Buddy 68, 140

L

Lawrence, Carol 135

Lee, Brenda 37, 39, 68, 93, 116, 120

Lee, Curtis 13

Leibowitz, Michael 14

Lemmon, Jack 69

Lennon, John 14, 25, 30, 34, 59, 93, 110-111, 117, 136, 153

Lettermen, The 35, 113, 139

Lewis, Bobby 6, 43, 159

Lewis, Garry 43

Lewis, Gary 139, 159

Lewis, Jerry 43, 107, 137, 155

Lewis, Jerry Lee 1, 10, 16, 34, 36, 78, 115, 149

Lewis, Jesse 121

Liberace 11

Libs, The Ad 134

Lockhart, June 132

Love, Mike 3, 94, 121, 145, 153

Lowry, Hunter 103, 106

Luke, Robin 121

Lulu 4, 45

Lundy, Steve 50

M

Man, Mr. Tambourine 1, 7

Mancini, Henry 128

Mann, Manfred 14, 63

Mantle, Mickey 132

March, Little Peggy 39

Margaret, Ann 65

Marie, Lisa 70

Martin, Dean 43, 56, 137, 155

Martin, George 134

Martin, Steve 59

Martinez, Rudy 3, 69

Marvelettes, The 20, 34, 109, 116

Mathis, Johnny 10, 21, 25, 89, 107, 142, 144, 152, 156

McCartney, Paul 11, 17, 34, 39, 46, 59, 94, 106, 110-111, 117, 152-153

McCoys, The 122

McGuinn, Roger 13, 139

McGuire, Barry 13

McLaughlyn, Marie McDonald 45

McPhatter, Clyde 48, 102, 118

McQuarrie, David 106

Melvin, Jesse 121

Memphis 1, 109, 116, 118

Michaels, John 50

Miller, Steve 123

Milsap, Ronnie 8

Moffatt, Tom 10, 57, 85, 101, 109, 116, 120-121

Monkeys 15, 17, 92, 109, 147-148

Monotones, The 126, 146

Monroe, Marilyn 124

Montez, Chris 107

Moon, Keith 136

Moondogs, Johnny and the 141

Morrison, Van 13, 15-16, 122

Motown 4, 39, 46, 81, 90, 109, 137

Mousekateer 68

Murmaids, The 13, 141

Murray, Anne 102, 151

N

Nash, Ruby 6

Nelson, Rick 37, 89, 102

Nelson, Rickey 155

Nelson, Ricky 60, 77

Neville, Aaron 19

Newton, Wayne 31, 85, 90, 132

Nicholson, Jack 22

Nightliners, The 67

Nightriders, The 27, 67, 102, 117

Nimoy, Leonard 124

Nixon, Richard 5, 31, 151

Norris, Marty 114

Nudy, Mr. 40

Nun, The Singing 141

O

Oates, John 152

Oop, Alley 90

Page 187

Index

Opry, Grand Ole 36, 39, 113, 149

Orbison, Roy 36, 40, 45, 62, 68, 85, 90-91, 98, 102, 156

Orchestra, The Electric Light 153

Orioles, Sonny Till and the 43

Osmond, Marie 45

Outsiders, The 113

P

Papas, The Mamas and 36

Park, Candlestick 36

Parker, Colonel 1, 32, 60, 70

Parker, Robert 54

Pendletones, The 122

Perkins, Anthony 47, 69

Perkins, Carl 1, 65

Pickett, Wilson 18, 58, 81, 83

Pitney, Gene 4, 13, 18, 54, 62, 69, 91, 100, 102, 114, 116, 127, 155-156

Platters 32, 85, 112

Platters, The 32, 112

Playboys, Garry Lewis and the 43

Preps, The Four 113

Presley, Elvis 1, 7-8, 10-11, 16, 20, 22, 28, 30-32, 36, 40, 43, 45-46, 49, 52, 56-60, 65, 70-74, 78-79, 89, 91, 100-102, 107, 110, 113, 115-116, 121, 127-128, 136-140, 149, 154-159

Presley, Gladys 72, 74

Price, Lloyd 9, 48

Q

Quarrymen, The 141

Quintet, The Sir Douglas 58, 78

R

Raiders 1, 134, 137

Raiders, The 1, 134, 137

Rascals, The 16, 57, 123

Rays, The 9, 31

Redding, Otis 45, 58, 83, 108, 122

Redford, Robert 84, 151

Reeves, Martha 45, 110, 120

Revere, Paul 1, 134

Revival, Creedence Clearwater 126

Reynolds, Debbie 65, 77

Ricardo, Ricky 137

Richard, Little 2, 10, 13-14, 34, 43, 45, 79, 107, 111, 115, 136, 156

Rivers, Johnny 44, 79, 89, 111, 116, 118, 120, 148-149

Rivileers, The 65

Rivilettes, The 65

Robinson, Smokey 6, 8, 23, 39-40, 46, 90, 108

Roe, Tommy 38, 45, 101, 135, 149

Rogers, Kenny 116, 118

Romantics, Ruby and the 54

Page 188

Index

Ron, Da Doo Ron 91

Ronnettes, The 36, 109

Ross, Diana 45, 81, 110

Ross, Dianna 22

Russell, Bobby 109

Russell, Leon 4, 11, 18

Rydell, Bobby 10, 67, 109

S

Sacco, Geno 54

Saints, Rocco and the 67

Sajak, Pat 125

School, Humes High 1

Scott, Jack 132

Scott, Linda 92

Seasons, Four 26, 31, 40, 49, 53, 62, 77, 82, 84, 113

Seasons, The Four 26, 31, 40, 49, 53, 62, 77, 82, 84, 113

Sebastion, John 15

Sedaka, Neil 4, 11, 13, 18, 23, 38, 48, 90, 102, 114

Sham, Sam The 13, 15, 17-18, 58

Shangrilas, The 20, 49

Shannon, Del 58

Sharp, Dee Dee 21, 110

Shaw, Rick 50

Shirelles, The 2, 20, 49, 53, 109, 130-131, 149, 156

Silhouettes, The 141

Simon, Carly 22, 151

Simon, Paul 29, 69

Sinatra, Frank 137

Sledge, Percy 138

Smith, Mike 136

Smith, Paul 136

Smith, Ricky 103, 106

Spector, Phil 13, 63, 109-110, 117, 134, 146, 154-156

Splash, Splish 125, 129, 136

Springfield, Dusty 119

Star, Richard 12

Starkey, Richard 12

Starkley, Richard 12

Starlighters, Joe Dee and the 41, 113

Starr, Richard 12

Starr, Ringo 12, 34, 39, 121, 159

Stephens, Ray 16

Stevens, Dan 127

Stevens, Dodie 109

Stewart, Billy 14-15

Stewart, Rod 122

Stills, Steven 15

Stones, The Rolling 36, 38, 41, 53, 82, 89, 122, 153, 156

Stookey, Noel Paul 13

Strait, George 8

Streisand, Barbara 22

Stroll, The 21, 112, 125

Sturgeoun, Tommy Lee 89

Sullivan, Ed 8, 58, 113, 128, 146

Summer, Donna 13

Supremes, The 4, 6, 8, 20, 38, 53, 57, 157

Swaggart, Jimmy 65

Swan, Billy 16

T

Taylor, James 22, 118, 151, 159

Teddybears, The 154, 156

Temptations, The 6, 46, 90

The Lovin' Spoonful 147

The O'Jays 15, 57

The Poni-Tails 126

Thomas, B.J. 16, 84-85

Tim, Tiny 14, 17, 28-29, 89, 122

Tokens, The 101

Tops, The Four 6, 46-47, 82, 113

Torrence, Dean 5

Trashmen, The 9

Trio, The Kingston 13, 36

Tripp, Scotty 50

Trivia, Captain 91, 100, 134

Trockmorton, Sonny 109

Turner, Tina 156

Turtles, The 27, 41, 57, 126, 147

Twilights, The 103

Twitty, Conway 8-9, 16, 34, 68, 77

Tyler, Frankie 52

V

Valens, Richie 69, 79

Valli, Franki 23, 52, 54, 62, 82

Valli, June 43

Vandellas, Martha and the 57

Vee, Bobby 100, 107, 139, 159

Velvets, The 146

Ventures, The 27, 141

Vibrations, The 122

Victors, The 122

Vincent, Gene 65

Vinton, Bobby 49, 89, 146

W

Waters, Muddy 154

Wayne, John 59, 124

Welby, Marcus 57

Welk, Lawrence 157

Wells, Mary 40, 46, 90, 110, 133

White, Andy 39

White, Edward H. 24

Who, The 64, 117, 122

Williams, Hank 2, 46

Williams, Larry 48, 79

Williams, Maurice 31, 82

Williams, Paul 141

Wilson, Brian 1, 3, 5-6, 9, 37, 54,

64, 90, 96, 121

Wilson, Carl 5, 18, 37, 64

Wilson, Dennis 64, 95

Wilson, Jackie 18, 58, 90, 128

Wonder, Stevie 5, 8, 23, 141, 148

Wood, Natalie 82

Wynette, Tammy 8

Y

Young, Bill 50

Young, Cathy 135

Young, Kathy 8, 65, 134

Z

Zicarro, Roby 114

Zodiacs, Maurice Williams and the
    31, 82

Zombies, The 101

Index

A Great Gift Idea!

Yes! I want to order _____ copies of *Pure Gold Rock & Roll Trivia Questions* by Ron Foster for only $14.95 + $1.95 postage & handling ($5.00 max). Texas residents add 8.25% sales tax.

Amount Enclosed:_____

METHOD OF PAYMENT

☐Check or money order (enclosed)

☐Credit Card ☐Visa ☐MasterCard ☐American Express

Card No. _____Expires _____

Signature_____

Phone _____

Name _____

Adress_____

City, State_____

Zip or Postal Code _____Country _____

Mail to:

Historical Publications, Inc.

15705 Hilcroft

Austin, Texas 78717-5331

(512) 255-4786

Or Fax: (512) 255-4789